How to write
a Thriller

If you want to know how . . .

Writing a Children's Book
'Rarely have I seen such well laid out advice and information –
don't take my word for it, buy a copy and see for yourself . . .
Highly recommended' – *Writers' Bulletin*

Creative Writing
'This is a book which merits a place on every writer's booklist'
– *Writers' Bulletin*

Writers' Guide to Copyright and Law
'Utterly invaluable . . . an absolute must for anyone putting pen to
paper for publication' – A reader, Leicestershire, UK

howtobooks

For full details, please send for a free copy
of the latest catalogue to:
How To Books
Spring Hill House, Spring Hill Road, Begbroke
Oxford OX5 1RX, United Kingdom
email: info@howtobooks.co.uk
www.howtobooks.co.uk

How to write a Thriller

SCOTT MARIANI

howtobooks

Published by How To Books Ltd,
Spring Hill House, Spring Hill Road,
Begbroke, Oxford OX5 1RX, United Kingdom.
Tel: (01865) 375794. Fax: (01865) 379162.
info@howtobooks.co.uk
www.howtobooks.co.uk

British Library Cataloguing in Publication Data.
A catalogue record for this book is available from
the British Library.

ISBN 978 1 84528 163 2

Produced for How To Books by Deer Park Productions, Tavistock
Cover design by Baseline Arts Ltd, Oxford
Typeset by Kestrel Data, Exeter, Devon
Printed and bound by Cromwell Press Ltd, Trowbridge, Wiltshire

NOTE: The material contained in this book is set out in good
faith for general guidance and no liability can be accepted
for loss or expense incurred as a result of relying on particular
circumstances on statements made in the book. Laws and
regulations are complex and liable to change, and readers should
check the current position with the relevant authorities before
making personal arrangements.

Contents

Acknowledgements

I would like to express my gratitude to the many thriller readers, the writers and publishing professionals who contributed their time and input to the writing of this book.

Special thanks to:

Lee Child, who despite an amazingly busy schedule was kind enough to find the time to share some of his wisdom; to Maggie Griffin for her dynamic efficiency; to my agent, Tim Bates, for all his valuable help and for puting up with me; to Nikki Read at How To Books for supporting the idea of this book; and to Darley Anderson for the best four words of encouragement I've ever heard: 'Good luck – it's needed'. (But did he mean the book was needed, or the luck was?)

Scott Mariani

Scott Mariani is the author of the thriller *The Fulcanelli Manuscript*, published by Robert Hale. He is an active member of International Thriller Writers (ITW), and is currently at work on his next thriller novel.

Introduction

SO YOU WANT TO WRITE A THRILLER?

Well, you probably do, or else you wouldn't be reading this. And the fact that you've picked up this book and started reading this page – whether you've taken the book home or whether you're standing browsing in a bookstore – shows that you're serious about it, too. The idea's in your head and it won't go away. This isn't just some nebulous dream or passing fancy for you. You've made a decision. You want to write a thriller, maybe more than one. And not just write them, but to see them launched and competitively marketed in what has now become the dominant and most exciting genre in commercial fiction publishing.

If that's the case, you can be justifiably proud for having set yourself such a worthy goal. But if you've come this far, you probably also have some idea of the challenge you're taking on. For many aspiring thriller authors, the problem isn't a lack of enthusiasm or energy, nor even a lack of brilliant talent bursting to get out and express itself on the page. It's knowing how to bridge that tremendous chasm that now opens up before you, the vast unknown gulf that lies between the first thrilling glimmer of an idea and actually seeing the finished novel in print where it belongs. If you are

1

standing on the edge looking across, wondering what it's going to take to get to the other side, this book is for you.

This book is written by someone who knows all too well what it takes to get a germ of an idea developed into a story and ultimately into a published thriller novel. I have travelled the rocky road (and made it to the end), and now I'd like to guide you to follow it successfully. It's a long journey through an unforgiving wilderness, and the way is littered with the bones of those who didn't make it. But you're determined not to let that happen to you. The fact that you're reading these words shows that.

Yes, it's a tough task. Yes, there will be moments along the way when you feel challenged and think about giving it up. But you rise to the challenge because of the golden treasure that lies at the end. *Your thriller novel, in print, in the shops, in the hands of readers.*

Many of those thriller writers who achieved their goal have struggled for years and made many false starts and wrong turns along the way, because there was nobody there to guide them. And many of those who didn't make it, gave up on their novel or finished it but never had the satisfaction of getting it into print, also failed not because they didn't have the right raw material, but because nobody showed them how to make the best of what they had. That's the harsh reality of this business. Even the most brilliant idea will end up in the trash if you don't know how to shape it, present it, and sell it. The aspiring thriller author owes it to themselves to learn the techniques and tricks that will help build and nurture that first fragile concept into a fully-developed and powerful novel. Venturing 'out there' into the highly competitive world of commercial fiction publishing isn't something to be done lightly, and if you want to have any chance of success at all you need to be as fully prepared as you can be. That's what this book aims to offer you.

The good news is that the majority of people already have the built-in potential to write a successful thriller. Why? Because you don't need to be a prodigy, a literary genius. All you really need is a love of your craft, a little imagination, a little inspiration, a pen in your hand or your fingers on the keys, bags of persistence and a solid understanding of the business. You *can* write a commercially-viable thriller, and sell it to the right market, if you are prepared to put in the effort and the time. You *can* learn to write flowing and exciting prose, create smart and zippy dialogue that crackles on the page, give birth to characters who will engage and enthral, and design twists and suspense that will have readers tearing out the pages in their haste to turn them . . . and maybe also have publishers tearing out their chequebooks in their haste to sign you up. You just need to know how.

This isn't a recipe book, nor is it a treasure map. There are no magic alchemical formulae on offer here, no secrets for instant success, no 'X marks the spot'. I'm not promising you that following the advice and ideas in this book will make you into a best-selling author. But what I *am* promising you is that if you do, you'll have a much better chance of achieving your goal. So, if you're still interested, let's go.

(1)

Beginnings

ART VERSUS COMMERCE

A lot of would-be authors talk about writing as though the creative act of composing a novel were an end in itself. Likewise, most of the self-help books intended to teach creative writing focus almost entirely on the artistic and literary elements of novel writing, and place little emphasis on the craft of designing a commercial product.

Ouch! What an awful word – *product*. Say it to your writing group, and the chances are you'll get to see at least some of them flinch. Yet that's exactly what a thriller is. Of course, there's an art to writing one – it's not a mechanistic, by-the-numbers process by any means. But then, there's also an art to designing a car, a TV advertisement or a bottle label. A commercial novel is a product, just like any other, and the reason I've started the first chapter of this book making this hard fact clear is that it may be the most important lesson you'll ever learn.

Looking in from the outside, you might think that art and business have always had an uneasy relationship. You'd be wrong, though, for art and business go together like peaches and cream. Think of it this way: Wolfgang Amadeus Mozart, one of the greatest composers who ever lived, might seldom have written a note of music if he hadn't spent most of his adult life worried about money and constantly trying to get commissions. The great English novelist, Anthony Trollope, came from an impoverished background and was very proud of the fact that his writing was earning him a good living. Like his contemporary, Charles Dickens, he was happy to sell his stories to newspaper editors to make money. Nowadays we think of the painter Vincent Van Gogh as the creator of some of the world's most valuable art – but in fact he was miserable and depressed all his life, and would probably have loved to make just one sale! The renaissance artist Michelangelo, would never have had the opportunity to paint what is arguably his greatest work, the famous Sistine chapel ceiling, if he hadn't been commissioned to do so by the Church. And the list goes on. None of these works of art are any less beautiful for having been born under economic pressure and designed according to commercial standards.

So you see, art and business have always been intertwined. Sure, there are writers for whom 'commercial' is a dirty word, who loudly declare that they write only for love and would never dream of debasing their literary creativity with any implication of financial gain. That's fine, and good luck to them. For the rest of us, whose prime interest is catering for a commercial market and perhaps even making something out of it, these are facts of life. It doesn't mean we love our craft any less. Nor does it mean that the thriller should be regarded in any way as a second-rate form of literature. This is a modern art form in its own right, and one that requires skill and dedication to master.

Childhood dream, adult business

Ever since she was a tiny child, Jane had a vivid storyteller's imagination. Even before she could read and write, she was wowing her parents with the way she could create imaginary characters and scenarios and play them out with her dolls and teddies. As soon as she could make the words on the paper, she was writing stories. At school her teachers encouraged her and told her she had the makings of a writer, and by the age of 15 that was all she wanted to do. But another 15 years went by, and she hadn't got a single word in print.

Why? Because although Jane grew up, her writing never grew up with her. All her life she'd been writing for herself, writing what *she* wanted to read. Storytelling had been part of her world for so long, she'd taken it for granted and never stopped to reassess her relationship with it. It never occurred to her that writing was a business. She'd failed to let her attitude to writing mature. The part of her that was a writer was still a child.

The writing world is full of people like Jane, who may have a brilliant imagination and perhaps even a great talent. But these hopefuls very often never see anything they've written get published, because they haven't learned the essential lesson. It may be a childhood dream, but writing is a business for grown-ups. The skills and attitude a writer needs are no different from those needed in any other competitive arena.

And it is *very* competitive. Of all the millions of people scribbling away trying to get published, only a tiny fraction of a per cent will ever make it. Even at the lower strata of the publishing industry, the broad base of the pyramid, things are tough – for instance, say you wanted to write a guidebook on pottery or country walks. You may know your subject like the back of your hand, but can you write about it interestingly, *commercially*? Even in this relatively gentle environment, you'll be up against loads of competition. Even a small publisher that only produces a dozen titles a year in a relatively uncompetitive market will easily receive over a thousand submissions. That's a lot of rejections, and a lot of disappointed would-be authors, to whittle the list down to 11 or 12.

It's tough at the top

If it's tough at the bottom, it's *seriously* tough at the top. The summit of the publishing industry is the multi-billion-dollar commercial fiction market. For a long time, the romantic novel was king of the heap, with publishers such as Mills & Boon boasting six or even seven-figure sales for every title they produced. It may have been the astonishing success of Dan Brown's runaway bestseller *The Da Vinci Code* that did it, but for whatever reason in 2005 a new champion emerged to take the crown – the commercial thriller. The revenues from this market are simply staggering, and because books are cheaper than ever to produce, the profits for publishers are better than the movie industry.

What does that mean for writers? Does it mean that publishers will throw money at every new wannabe who comes along, in the hope that their novel will become the Next Big Thing? Sadly not. What it *does* mean is that the market is becoming increasingly flooded with submissions from hopeful writers with their eye on the bestseller list.

While the publishers can afford to churn out many titles each year to satisfy the enormous public demand, the number of fledgling authors trying to get a piece of the action is now so disproportionately huge that the competition is through the roof. If this were a war, even the most hardened general would blanch at the casualty rate.

Sounds terrible, doesn't it? Well, don't panic. The good news is that a very great many of those wannabe thriller authors were in such a hurry to get in the door that they didn't stop to think about what they were doing. You can even the odds considerably by first making sure that you're getting it right, and that is what this book intends to help you with.

THE JOB OF THE THRILLER WRITER

The thriller writer's task is essentially a simple one. Your job, in the same vein as your cousin the horror writer, is to provide the reader with – as the name of our chosen genre suggests – *thrills*. You are providing them with an experience. Your reader buys your book in the same spirit that they might buy a movie ticket or a ride on a roller-coaster. They want to be entertained. They want to be thrilled. They want you to take them somewhere exciting where they've never been before.

So really, that's all it's about. A thriller writer doesn't need to have much in the way of literary pretensions – as a matter of fact these may be more of a hindrance than a help. You don't need to be especially fancy with words or be conversant with the finer points of literary technique. You don't have to be highly educated, and you don't even need to be particularly well-schooled in literature as long as you have a pretty keen idea of the market in which you'll be competing. You simply want to tell the story in such a way as to hit them hard and keep them turning the pages, compulsively, feverishly, until, somewhere on a beach or in a hotel room in some distant land, or sitting in a plane high over the Atlantic, or propped up in bed in the middle of the night long after everyone else has gone to sleep, your thoroughly satisfied reader drinks down the last line of your book, closes the covers and breathes 'Wow . . . that was great'.

Have I got it in me?

Have you ever read, or watched, a thriller and found yourself thinking something like:

◆ 'That was a really good idea, but it would've been better if . . .'.

◆ 'There were good parts to it, but they didn't do a great job of it. Here's how *I* would have done it . . .'.

◆ 'Hey, that gives *me* an idea for something that's never been done before!'.

Or have you ever read something in a magazine and thought 'gosh, that would make a good story for a thriller'? Have you ever stood looking in the bookshop window, nose pressed to the glass and gazing at the rows of new titles and thought 'I want to be there'?

If so, the chances are that yes, you *have* got it in you, if you're prepared to work at it. If the raw material is there, and the desire is there, all you need to do is put in the work . . . lots and lots of it.

FACING THE CHALLENGE

As well as a realistic attitude about this business, another extremely important asset for the beginning writer is confidence. Don't let yourself be intimidated by the scope of what you're taking on. Remind yourself that even the most successful authors, the names in the bestseller lists, were once standing where you are standing now, looking up at the looming mountain above them with the same sense of trepidation. They achieved their goal, and you're going to have a damn good crack at it too.

Don't be put off by friends or relatives who laugh or joke about your ambition to write a thriller. One of my writer friends was kindly told by his brother that he had more chance of winning the lottery than ever getting a book published. He is now a published author several times over, and has yet to win a penny on the lottery.

If it helps, watch inspiring movies to boost your sense of self-confidence. This is not such a corny thing to do – and actually you can learn a lot along the way by observing how master storytellers can inspire their audiences. There are hundreds of films which, even if the storylines are completely irrelevant to your personal quest, deal with the universal theme of the struggle of the little guy overcoming adversity. *Wimbledon*, *Rocky* (the first one), *Hidalgo*, *Educating Rita*, are all about people who faced up to challenges, refused to accept their limitations, overcame the odds, not only to achieve their ambitions but to flourish as human beings.

Read the memoirs and biographies of successful people, not necessarily writers – people like Tiger Woods and Arnold Schwarzenegger, and think about what personal qualities these people must have had to enable their success. You'll find that the themes are the same as those inspiring movies: it's the dedication, resolve and persistence of these real or imagined characters that sees them through. Learn to feel that sense of fierce determination flowing through your own veins, and allow yourself to feel fired up by it.

HONING YOUR WRITING CRAFT

It's also important to develop a good writing style. Take the time and put in the effort to learn the techniques of effective writing. In this regard, published thriller novels should be your main training ground. Most people read them passively, letting their eyes skim over the words. They read books in the same way that you or I would drink a glass of wine – just for enjoyment and relaxation. But think of how an expert wine taster drinks wine, savouring the flavour, analysing its constituents, critically comparing it to other wines they have tasted. You should train yourself to read thrillers in just the same way as the wine taster drinks wine – actively and rigorously. Why did the author use that word? Look at the way he structured that sentence. Look how that dialogue flowed. If a piece of writing grabs, excites or moves you, don't just enjoy it and move on. Go back and study *why* it did. How did it work? Don't just read the words, put yourself in the author's place and imagine yourself writing the words. How does that feel? How would you have done it differently?

Start putting these lessons into practice in your own writing. Don't try too hard to ape the styles of your favourite authors, or your writing will be flat and toneless. When reading your own writing critically, learn to hit the right balance – be honest about your weaknesses, but not so ruthlessly self-critical as to undermine your confidence.

As this book progresses, we'll be delving in depth into the innermost workings of the thriller, probing inside the machinery to see how it all hangs together and how it effects its impact on the reader. Applying the ideas we explore to the thriller novels in your expanding collection (or so it should be!) will help you to develop an increasing grasp of how it all works in practice. I urge you not to get too hung up about it for the moment.

Reading books on writing

I'm not going to come down hard on books that purport to teach you to write – after all, I'm the author of this one! By all means, read as much as you can to help you learn about the process of becoming a writer, learning to write well, and so on. But read sensibly and with discrimination. One current writer's self-help guide lists as recommended reading a number of books written as far back as 1927 (E.M. Forster's *Aspects of the Novel*). While such books may offer fascinating historical insights into what was once involved in writing a novel, their value to an aspiring novelist in the twenty-first century is very open to question. So much has changed since then – writing styles, our language itself, technology and the media, lifestyle, and society as a whole. You would be far better off concentrating instead on the books your peers in the thriller business are writing. If you can train yourself to read them actively and critically as mentioned above – and as this book will help you to do – you won't need much else in the way of book resources.

Kindred spirits: joining a writers' group

It's true that writing is a pretty solitary business. If that bothers you, you may be drawn to a local writers' group or circle. Most towns have one, and you should be able to find out whom to contact from the library. Information on writers' groups is also to be found in *The Writer's Handbook*, a very useful publication that we'll be coming back to later.

You may find joining such a group extremely beneficial, but consider the following cautionary tale:

Sally, a young would-be writer of fiction, thought it would be a good idea to meet up with some like-minded people, discuss books together and maybe gain some inspiration. She found out about a local writing group and attended one of their monthly meetings. None of the people in the circle had ever had anything published, but that didn't concern Sally. When she arrived, she introduced herself and explained to the group that she was in the middle of writing her first novel. But the group's initial murmur of enthusiasm soon evaporated into stony silence when Sally went on to describe what she was writing.

'What did you say?' one of them asked, wrinkling her nose in distaste. 'You're writing a . . . *what* novel?' exclaimed another lady, almost dropping her coffee cup. Sally was a little bemused by the response. 'I said I'm writing a *commercial* novel', she repeated hesitantly. 'A thriller'. Nobody spoke another word to Sally after that, and she never returned to the group.

What went wrong? From the group's reaction, it was as though she had come out with some gross obscenity. And in fact, from their point of view, she had! She had unwittingly blurted out the 'c' word – *commercial*.

Unfortunately, the writers' group Sally had chanced upon weren't really writers at all. They just *thought* they were. Their idea of what it is to be a writer was radically different from mine, from yours if you're still reading this, and from every professional author out there.

You may be lucky and find a writers' group that is genuinely interested in real writing and not wrapped up in arty, snobbish pseudo-literary affectations. However, I'd suggest that if you can't find a group with the right attitude, you're probably better off going it alone. They'll only take the wind out your sails, treat you like an alien and waste your time. Alternatively, start your own group with other people who are serious about getting commercial fiction into print.

PENCIL OR PC: FINDING A MEDIUM THAT WORKS FOR YOU

Whether you decide to opt for the traditional chewed pencil and A4 pad, the charming old-fashioned typewriter or a state-of-the-art laptop, is really up to you. Many writers have very strong preferences one way or the other, and would find themselves unable to write a word on any other medium. It's very much a question of personal choice. Do remember, though, that your typescript will have to be as professionally and neatly presented as possible – no publisher or agent will look at a dog-eared scrawl, and will immediately assume that the poor standard of presentation will be reflected in sloppy writing and an unprofessional attitude generally. If you prefer to work on paper alone, you'll either have to type the whole thing up on a computer later or get someone to do it for you.

The word processor as a dynamic writing tool

Don't think of it as a soulless symbol of deadened artistic values, think of it as the most flexible tool that human technology has ever given to the writer. A computer is not a writer, and isn't magically going to transform you into a literary genius – the adage of 'rubbish in, rubbish out' was never truer. But having used one myself for quite a few years, I have to say I could not be without it and cannot even imagine how people coped in the days of clunky old type-writers, ink ribbons and correcting fluid. A fast modern machine using software like the trusty Word 2003 I'm using now is truly a beautiful tool and brings a whole new creative dimension to the process of putting a book together.

The computer is to the writer what the modern digital editing suite is to a film director. I love the way I can zip chunks of text around and play with the form, experimenting to find what's most effective. Whole chapters can be moved around at will, scenes can be intercut or exchanged at the flick of a key. The word search facility is a blessed aid to maintaining continuity in an ever-evolving sinuous storyline – just type in a keyword and you can trawl through a 500-page document in seconds to find the bits you need to change. If you decide to alter the name of a character, it can be done almost instantly by using the search/replace all facility. Imagine the chore of altering 'Charlie' to 'Tom' 2,000 times with correcting fluid! You can also highlight pieces of text in other colours if you're not sure about them – I use blue to signify 'to be revised' and red for anything that is only a suggestion or an experimental idea thrown in.

The computer is, or can be, an integral part of the creative process. It allows you to build and grow your novel like a living creature, starting with a basic framework or skeleton and watching it swell and take shape as you 'inject' scenes into it at whichever point you choose. At its best, it can almost be a pure extension of your imagination, allowing you to throw out creative ideas and meld them fluidly into an organic whole. It also offers you the benefit of near-instant communication. If sending work in to your agent or making a pitch to a publisher, it takes seconds to attach text to an email and pop it through to them. Do check first that they will accept email submissions – many still don't, although this can change once you have a good working relationship with them.

Protecting yourself against lost data

If there's a downside to using a computer to write on, it's that you are entrusting your increasingly precious document to a bunch of electronics. Should anything happen to your machine, you could lose everything. You need to think of ways to protect yourself from going completely insane with grief in the event of such a disaster. It pays to become obsessive about regularly copying the latest version of your work-in-progress onto CD, as well as keeping hard (printed) copies of anything you would like to keep. You may end up spending money on printer cartridges and paper, but it's worth it for safety's sake. It's also quite nice to be able to take your work away from the desk and read it else-where, say in the comfort of your living room where new ideas may come to you. Then you can jot these down on the printout, and later return to the computer to make the changes.

Other useful equipment

Even if you're a techno-junkie who depends entirely on the computer to write on, there are bits and bobs of other equipment that you may still find useful. I would advise you always to carry a little notebook around with you, in case the muse should unexpectedly strike. Don't kid yourself that the brilliant idea that occurred to you ten minutes ago will still be clear in your mind five hours later. Like dreams, they slip away. Catch them in your net.

Some writers like to record ideas either on tape or a more modern digital recording device. Although you may get some funny looks on the underground when you suddenly pull out your recorder and proceed to announce your fiendish new idea for the best way to bump off one of your characters!

FINDING THE TIME AND THE PLACE TO WRITE

Time distractions (children, work, shopping and other chores) and noise distractions (children again, TV, barking dogs, noisy neighbours) can seriously intrude on a writer's ability to work productively. Time management is more a critical issue for some writers than for others. Some budding writers can afford to take time off work or go part-time for a while, others are happy to work late nights and week-ends, and others just accept that their progress will be slow. Partners and spouses may be willing to take on extra duties such as ferrying children, cooking and shopping, etc. – but don't, please, risk your marital harmony for the sake of your novel!

If working at home is too noisy and full of distractions, you may be able to find somewhere else to retreat to. Roald Dahl had his garden shed, Patrick O'Brian his vineyard. Working in the library is a possible option, although if like me you're a messy sort of writer who quickly surrounds himself with mountains of books and papers that spread out to take over the whole room, your presence may not be welcome. You may be able to rent a cheap office some-where, or even beg a friend to let you invade an unused attic space or spare bedroom. That's one thing this book can't really help you with!

Workshop for Chapter 1

At the end of each chapter of the book, I'll list some practical things for you to try out. The exercises below are intended to get you started thinking like a thriller writer, and are based on the kind of assignments I give my students at writing workshops and courses.

➢ Go to your local bookshop and look at the thriller section. Spend an hour browsing through different ones. Take note of when they were written (every book has a publishing history printed on the first page). Take note of who the most successful or prolific writers are, what kind of thrillers they write and who publishes them.

➢ Read a thriller. Buy a recent one if you can afford it, or borrow from a friend. A thriller borrowed from the local library or bought cheap in a second-hand stall may be too old and its subject matter out of fashion.

➢ Think, objectively and in detail, what it was about this thriller that you liked – or didn't like. Bear in mind that if you didn't like it but six million readers still bought it, you need to be even more objective! Why was the book successful? What could you learn from it?

➢ Start browsing through newspapers and magazines and actively thinking about ideas for your own thriller.

The Idea

As Bruce Springsteen sang, 'you can't light a fire without a spark'. That elusive spark is the starting point from which all thrillers are born. Every great story originates from some simple idea that gestates and evolves in the writer's mind, slowly building up into a tight and sophisticated plot with all the right elements in place. The initial idea could be to do with a character around whom a storyline later develops, or it could be a basic storyline idea into which characters are later placed. Very seldom will the whole package drop into your lap in one go!

INSPIRATION (AND HOW NOT TO SCARE IT AWAY)

It's almost impossible for even the most experienced writer to conjure up a great idea out of the blue without it seeming forced. The best, most truly inspired ideas are the ones that find *you*.

Inspiration is an elusive thing. Like a sensitive wild animal – a deer, or a bird – it will tend to flee from you if you try to approach it. The more you press yourself on it, the more it will run or fly away from you. It's only when you stop chasing it, and can relax and sit quietly, that the animal may approach you in its own time and let you share its space.

Closing your fingers on a fleeting idea is also like trying to remember a dream. The more you try to focus on the fading memory, the more it seems to elude you. Then, later, when you've stopped trying so hard to remember, it may pop into your mind clear as crystal.

Let it flow

As your ideas begin to come to you, let them flow gently and freely. Don't sit staring at an empty screen or a blank page, waiting for it all to fit into place – you can't force it. You'll only get bogged down and frustrated and any ideas you do get will tend to be forced and contrived. Only when your mind is relaxed and the atmosphere right, will it all begin to flow. Some writers find that their best ideas come to them while walking in the country, riding a bicycle or even mowing the lawn. So again, don't chase it, let it come to you.

The trigger

A brilliant idea for a thriller novel could hit you at any time. It may be that it's already there, half-formed in your unconscious; or maybe it's lurking just around the corner waiting to zap you. Anything could trigger it off:

◆ Something you read in a magazine or see in a movie.

◆ A news item on the TV or radio.

◆ A conversation over breakfast or with a stranger.

◆ A recollection of something that happened to you long ago.

◆ Some seemingly trivial event that occurs at work or on holiday, on a plane or a train or anywhere at all.

Whatever it is, and however it comes, you should be ready to spot it, catch it and store it away safely. As mentioned in the previous chapter, keep a notebook handy so that you can scribble things down as they come to you. You might want to keep one under the pillow, just in case inspiration should strike in the middle of the night or during that twilight zone between sleep and waking when the mind seems to produce some of its most vivid ideas. If you are the kind of writer who insists on keeping writing implements in the bed, just don't spear yourself with your pencil in your sleep, as happened to one writer who shall remain nameless.

RESOURCES FOR IDEAS

Let's get one thing clear right now, shall we? There is no Idea Dump, no Story Central, no Island of the Buried Bestsellers; good story ideas seem to come quite literally from nowhere, sailing at you right out of the empty sky . . . Your job isn't to find these ideas but to recognise them when they show up.

On Writing, Stephen King

He's right, of course, but there *are* places you can trawl around and often find that germ of an idea, that scrap of loose information that strikes the spark in your brain and may be the origin of what eventually evolves into a strong original story.

Part of the inspiration for my thriller *The Fulcanelli Manuscript* came from an article in *New Scientist* magazine, which described the rise of religious fundamentalism across the world. I recommend this popular science magazine very strongly as a fantastic resource for plot ideas – the scientific information is reliable and responsible, yet accessible to non-scientists and, as it's a mass-market publication, appealing to a wide audience without ever being sensationalistic.

As I write, I'm flipping through a couple of issues of *New Scientist* on my desk. Even in just a few pages I'm seeing all kinds of ideas that could work really well in a thriller:

◆ Dire warnings about killer viruses like bird flu – this is all very topical stuff and rich ground for the thriller writer.

◆ Plans to start mining the mineral-rich rock of asteroids within a few more years – brilliant scope for all kinds of double-dealing, corruption and skulduggery with a difference.

◆ Drug companies producing drugs to suppress memory – great potential for shady government agencies to misuse these!

◆ Questions about the safety of scientific developments, e.g. GM crops – eco-thrillers and cover-ups are still popular with readers.

◆ Did you know that, according to Einstein's theories, if you made something fly faster than the speed of light you could theoretically destroy the universe? The 'mad scientist' theme still has some meat on it after all these years – though beware of corny Quatermass-type stuff.

Other popular science magazines can be useful too. Leafing through an issue of *The Sky at Night* I find:

◆ Astronomical mysteries of the pyramids.

◆ Constellations that form a stellar map pointing to a hidden ancient secret.

◆ Was Stonehenge an early astronomical lab with a buried secret to reveal? (Yes, Stonehenge is a pretty cheesy subject – but so are many others that are nonetheless brought back to life by imaginative writers – it's how you do it that matters!).

All these are potentially useful ideas. In fact, once your eye is tuned to them, you'll see brilliant ideas everywhere you look: newspapers, history books, TV documentaries, museums – the list is endless.

KNOW THE GENRE

While your baby thriller is gestating in your mind, it's important to keep a close eye on the market you're aiming to cater for. What 'know the genre' really means for the writer is '*know what people out there are buying, and what you should be trying to sell to a publisher or literary agent*'. In the first instance, you'll be selling your idea to them, not to the public. Make no mistake, those people are a lot harder to please than the public! And the best way to know in advance whether your idea is going to please the gods is to compare it with what has gone – and made money – before. Another vital reason for studying your genre is simply in order to know whether your idea, however exciting it may be to you, is just another tired re-tread of an old cliché. It pays to get used to, early on, the painful act of scrunching up your whole basic premise and throwing it away, because you'll be doing a lot more scrunching up later on.

Sub-genres

Be aware of the different sub-genres within the thriller genre, and see where yours fits in. Many thrillers mix these genres up, of course, but the basic types include:

◆ **The adventure thriller**
   (*Polar Shift* and *Lost City*, Clive Cussler)

◆ **The espionage thriller**
   (*The Cell*, Colin Forbes; *The Teeth of the Tiger*, Tom Clancy; *The Sigma Protocol* and the Jason Bourne novels by Robert Ludlum)

◆ **The cops and crooks thriller**
   (*L.A. Confidential*, James Ellroy; *Out of Sight*, Elmore Leonard; *Hostage*, Robert Crais)

◆ **The historical mystery/conspiracy/hidden treasure thriller**
   (*The Rule of Four*, Ian Caldwell and Dustin Thomason; *The Da Vinci Code*, Dan Brown; *Map of Bones*, James Rollins; *The Assassini*, Thomas Gifford)

◆ **The legal/political thriller**
   (*The Client*, John Grisham; *The Constant Gardener*, John Le Carré; *Family Claims*, Twist Phelan; *Past Caring*, Robert Goddard; *Split Second*, David Baldacci)

◆ **The murder/'whodunnit' thriller**
(*Into the Blue*, Robert Goddard; *Complicity*, Iain Banks; *A Taste for Death*, P.D. James; *The Dead House*, Linda Fairstein; *Predator*, Patricia Cornwell)

◆ **The psychological thriller**
(*Promise Me*, Harlan Coben; *The Stranger House*, Reginald Hill; *Misery*, Stephen King)

◆ **The quasi-horror thriller**
(*Firestarter*, Stephen King; *The Devil's Advocate*, Andrew Neiderman)

◆ **The techno-scientific thriller**
(*Digital Fortress*, Dan Brown; *The Genesis Code*, John Case; *Prey*, Michael Crichton; *Nemesis*, Bill Napier)

◆ **The military/shoot 'em up thriller**
(*Die Trying*, Lee Child; *The Act of War*, Dale Brown; *Hunter Killer*, Patrick Robinson; *The Hijack*, Duncan Falconer)

Here today, gone tomorrow

It's important to bear in mind that fashions change and the hot idea that spawns a score of bestsellers one year may have cooled off significantly by the next. Writing is just about writing; publishing is about timing. Even a brilliantly-written thriller serving up yesterday's reheated dinner is unlikely to excite publishers.

The topicality of a thriller is very much tied to the ebb and flow of world events. Look how dated all those

Cold-War-era period pieces seem now. At one time, thriller baddies were often rogue KGB agents or IRA terrorists. In the wake of the events of '9/11', the bombings in Madrid and London and the currently imminent danger of further terror strikes in Europe and the USA, the eyes of the Western world have become fixed on a new threat. It may be that in a few more years, those tensions will have diminished and we will have found fresh enemies to fear. Whatever happens, savvy thriller writers will always have one eye glued to the media and their finger on the public's pulse.

You need not only to be aware of what the big stories are now; to a certain degree you need to be able to anticipate what will still be 'hot' when your book appears. This isn't an easy task, considering that the journey from initial idea to published novel may take two, even three years: a year or more to write and develop it, months or even a year while agents and editors make you hack away at it, and then a lengthy delay while it goes through the wheels of the publishing process. Don't chase the current fashion, think ahead.

One way to avoid the 'yesterday's news' syndrome is to concentrate on universal human themes that never die: tales of corruption, the innocent victim, races against time, kidnap dramas, psychological thrillers, all remain evergreen.

KNOW THE RULES

You will often hear writers insisting that there are no rules to writing a novel. Well, that can be the case at the more literary end of the scale, but in fact there are some basic rules and conventions that govern the thriller genre, and which you ignore at the risk of getting turned down everywhere you take your manuscript.

The supreme golden rule is that the thriller must at all times keep the reader wanting to turn the page. As one leading literary agent put it to me:

> Imagine the reader as someone who wants to get away from the book, to put it down. It's your job to make sure they are unable to do that.

A thriller must always carry a sense of risk and danger, whether it deals with a 'cast of thousands', such as a whole population in jeopardy, or takes a more intimate approach with only one or two people in danger. Here, more is not necessarily better: the reader will often be able to empathise more with a single person at risk than an anonymous million residents of some city threatened with disaster.

What publishers and agents want from a thriller:

◆ A story that commands attention right from the start and holds it to the end.

◆ Pace and excitement, keeping the reader wondering what's going to happen next.

◆ Lots of twists, thrills, suspense and unexpected developments.

◆ Believable characters that will engage the reader – if you can't make them care about the characters or what happens to them, you've lost it.

What readers want from a thriller

The following comments are selected from a group of 20 thriller fans, ten men and ten women, who were asked to sum up the things they look for in a book:

◆ *'A gripping story with lots of mystery and intrigue.'*

◆ *'A believable, intelligent plot.'*

◆ *'I like a plot that keeps me guessing, when I can't tell how it's going to end up.'*

◆ *'A likeable main character, someone I can relate to.'*

◆ *'Plenty of action and drama.'*

◆ *'Something that takes me out of my dull life and into a world of fantasy!'*

◆ *'I do a lot of travelling, and I like a thriller that will keep me engaged for long periods while sitting on trains and in airport lounges.'*

◆ *'Fast pace, interesting storylines, lots of exotic locations.'*

◆ *'Plain old simple storytelling – I can't stand those books that are so complicated you can't remember what's going on.'*

◆ *'A sexy, strong hero – someone you feel safe with.'*

◆ *'Pure entertainment – I'm not interested in anything with a message!'*

WHO AM I WRITING FOR?

The amateur writer is someone who writes for themselves. A professional writer is someone who writes for other people.

This is not to say that you shouldn't be passionately involved with your idea. If your thriller is something you yourself would want to read, and you'd be one of the horde beating down the bookstore door to get a copy, so much the better. Indeed, if you're anything less than passionate about your writing, it will show. But you've also got to remain objective, and always bear your audience in mind.

Some tough questions!

From the earliest stages of writing your story, you should be getting into the mindset of the agents and publishers, and asking yourself the questions they will eventually be asking you:

◆ What is so special about your story?

◆ How does it stand out from the crowd?

◆ Why should anyone want to invest money in publishing and promoting it?

◆ What is the target audience for this book?

◆ What other books do they already read?

◆ Why would they want to read yours?

◆ What makes you qualified or suited to writing this book?

◆ What have you, as an individual, got that others haven't got?

If you think these questions are tough and brutal, you're right! But face up to it, because this is exactly the kind of impersonal scrutiny you'll be receiving later on from the hard-nosed business folks, the people with the money, the ones who make the decisions. The more openly you address these questions now:

◆ the better thought-out your idea will be, and
◆ the better you'll be able to pitch it later on.

BOOK AND FILM

Thriller novels and thriller movies have a very close relationship. The same elements are needed to make them successful: pace, excitement, strong characters, gripping storylines with lots of twists and turns.

Technical differences apart, ultimately a thriller novel and a thriller movie are exactly the same thing, just working in a different medium. That's why so many film producers keep a sharp eye on the thriller fiction world, looking out for a property that could translate well into a commercially successful movie. For them, books are a kind of 'poor man's film' – relatively cheap to produce and a great way of testing the waters to see how a story will appeal to the public before going and investing a hundred million dollars into it! If a novel is popular, there's a good chance the film will be too. So, in a very real sense, when you get into writing thrillers you are also potentially entering the wonderful world of the silver screen.

Book-to-film adaptations

Next time you're browsing through the video store, read the small print on the back of some DVDs and take note of how many thrillers have been adapted from novels. This has been going on forever – one early example of a thriller novel making it to celluloid is the 1935 Hitchcock rendition of *The Thirty-Nine Steps*, (fairly loosely) based on the John Buchan novel. Another classic book-to-film adaptation is *Strangers on a Train*, based on the novel by Patricia Highsmith and directed, again, by the great Hitchcock. Some more recent examples are *The Bourne Identity/Bourne Supremacy* (adapted from Robert Ludlum's Jason Bourne novels), *The Constant Gardener* (a great conspiracy thriller based on the book by John Le Carré), *First Blood* (adapted from the original novel by David Morrell), *Absolute Power* (directed by and starring Clint Eastwood, based on a David Baldacci novel), Eastwood's *Blood Work* (based on a novel by Michael Connelly), and of course *The Da Vinci Code*.

So in short, don't feel guilty about spending a lot of time sitting watching movies. As long as you keep a part of your mind objective and *observe* what you're seeing from a story-teller's point of view, learning to analyse what works and what doesn't, it is in fact fantastic training for any thriller writer to see how these professionals set up effective story-lines, lay out the pace and create tension and suspense. Many DVDs contain a treasure-trove of special features, such as feature-length commentaries from directors and (better still) scriptwriters. Delve into these, as some of them can be extremely fascinating and highly educational.

THE THEMES BEHIND THE STORY

Every story, no matter what it's about, relates a sequence of events that happen to people. If you were to remove the human element, the whole thing would crumble and become meaningless – after all, we are humans and we want to read about things that affect our own kind. So behind every storyline there are themes that enrich it with universal meaning, themes such as love, endeavour, good versus evil, sacrifice, redemption, guilt, jealousy: a whole range of powerful notions we all recognise. Every story, however intriguing as a stand-alone idea, needs to hang on human themes embodied and played out by believable characters. As an example, it was the doomed love affair between the Leonardo DiCaprio and Kate Winslet characters in the film *Titanic* that made this story compelling and thrilling despite the fact that we all knew exactly what was going to happen.

Although at this stage your main concern is sketching out the basic idea, your mind should never be far from your characters. Even at this early point in the thriller's development, you should be thinking of three basic character areas:

1. The goodie – this includes the hero/heroine and any players along the way who help him/her.
2. The baddie – often the most interesting character – make him or her as villainous as possible but without sacrificing believability.
3. The love interest – almost every story has some kind of romantic element that adds an extra dimension to the main plot, or from which the plot hangs.

Some general universal plot themes

Look at most thrillers and you'll see many of the same themes emerging again and again. This doesn't mean they're repetitive and boring – it means that these are basic themes which, well handled, never fail to grip readers.

◆ **Someone has something that someone else wants**
Typically this is money, although it could also involve power intrigues, control of secret weapons, crimes of passion, grudges where someone feels cheated or overstepped, and many other possible scenarios.

◆ **Someone has information or knowledge that someone else doesn't want them to have**
An interesting additional twist is when the person in possession of that information – whatever it might be – doesn't *know* they have it, or doesn't understand its significance and has to figure things out while the baddies are on their trail. The dangerous information could be anything from a lost memory (e.g. in *The Bourne Identity*), to something planted on an innocent victim. The ensuing chase is often much more exciting than the import of the information itself.

◆ **Someone has witnessed something that makes them a threat to someone**
The 'witness in danger' scenario is a variation on the above – maybe they know the identity of a killer, or they have witnessed a high-level plot or some other piece of skulduggery (e.g. *Absolute Power*, where the hero witnesses a murder carried out on behalf of the US President).

◆ **Someone is planning to do something terrible, and someone else (the hero) must stop them**
  This is the standard cover-all format for many thrillers,
  from James Bond to Jack Reacher, cops and robbers,
  terrorist stories, serial killers and a thousand others.
  What qualifies the hero to save the day? It might be their
  super-skills and training, or like the *Da Vinci Code* hero
  Robert Langdon, they might have some sort of
  specialised knowledge that makes them the only person
  able to prevent catastrophe. Quite often we don't initially
  know what terrible things are being planned, or by
  whom. The hero, who may have come into the situation
  accidentally – a reporter, a detective, or just an ordinary
  member of the public – uncovers the truth by gradual
  steps, leading to: (a) the horrible realisation of what's
  going to happen, and (b) the race to prevent it. A great
  example of this set-up is *The First Horseman* by John
  Case, where reporter Frank Daly uncovers a terrible
  secret in the course of his investigations. Another is *The
  Assassini* by Thomas Gifford, where a brother in-
  vestigating his sister's mysterious death uncovers another
  dangerous secret.

RESEARCH AND AUTHENTICITY

Thrillers should have a solid ring of authenticity about them,
especially if you plan to venture into specialised territory
such as:

◆ Police/crime
◆ Medical/forensic

◆ Military

◆ Scientific/technological

Many successful thriller authors have extensive personal experience of the things they write about – for instance, John Grisham and David Baldacci come from high-powered legal backgrounds, Andy McNab and Chris Ryan are former SAS soldiers, and David Morrell (a former literature professor who created the Rambo franchise) has received military special forces training. Former jockeys such as Dick Francis and John Francome have specialised in race-based thrillers, ex-cops have written crime thrillers, former politicians have blown the whistle on the world of corruption and dirty tricks (and who better qualified than they?). These people all know their stuff thoroughly, and through them their readers will have acquired a certain level of authentic knowledge. By displaying a lack of knowledge you will appear sloppy and lose your reader's trust.

While you don't necessary have to have extensive personal experience to be able to write well and convincingly about a given subject, the less you know about it the more you must try to compensate with thorough research.

Firearms and weapons
Firearms and weapons come into thrillers quite a lot, and so if you don't know anything about them you may have to learn something. David Morrell is one author with obvious firearms knowledge, helping him to lend an authentic touch to his thrillers. As a former pistol coach, I find it irritating when writers clearly haven't bothered to do their homework on this subject! True, many readers won't know – or care –

that a single-action semi-automatic pistol doesn't go 'click' when fired empty, or that the correct name for a silencer is a sound suppressor, or what 'cocked and locked' means; you can easily get too pedantic on this subject and some writers have bordered on gun-fetishism. However, in a genre where authenticity and intensive research count for a great deal, writers who fail to check their details stand to lose credibility with hard-core thriller fans. And word spreads fast . . .

Technological information

Technological information must be up to date – for instance, electronic surveillance has come a long way since the days of planting microphones in telephone receivers. Bombs are no longer bundles of gelignite strapped to a ticking alarm clock. Modern readers, and especially younger people, are extremely conversant with computer technology, email and mobile phones. (Mobile phones are actually a fantastic story-telling device, offering all kinds of possibilities that were undreamed of in the days when characters had to go running from one phone booth to another.) So you need to overcome any technophobic tendencies, do your homework and don't be lazy!

Historical material

Any historical material you might want to incorporate into your thriller should be well researched. Naturally it's permissible to tweak historical truth a little, especially if dealing with ancient history – just look at *The Da Vinci Code* – but in general you should try to get your facts reasonably straight in order for the story to ring true, as well as to avert the wrath and ridicule of the critics. If you've based your story in a historical period, say the 1920s, find out what life was like then. How did people talk? What cars were around? What movies or plays were in the theatres? What names were up in lights – Buster Keaton? Charlie Chaplin? What did people wear? What songs were popular? What was topical and fashionable? Add in just enough background to create the right atmosphere, but don't overdo it as superfluous detail will slow the pace down and bore the reader.

Key research resources
Key research resources include:

1. Books
A well-chosen collection of specialised non-fiction titles can be a great research asset. For instance, a writer of crime thrillers would do well to invest in an up-to-date guide on current forensic testing methods. Legal books, psychology manuals, medical dictionaries, travel books, foreign phrase-books, may all be useful depending on what you write. For writers of thrillers involving military, combat, hostage rescue and personal security themes, a very useful reference and completely authentic source of information is the series of books by Mark V. Lonsdale. These include *Sniper Counter Sniper* and *Close Quarter Battle*, are published by the Specialised Tactical Training Unit (STTU) in the USA and are available at website: www.sttu.com. Buying any kinds of books can be expensive, but remember that you can offset their cost against tax later on once you start getting paid as a writer.

2. Libraries

However, make sure non-fiction material is recent and up to date, not some dusty old book from 1972 that will mislead you with antediluvian information.

3. The internet

Always make use of bona fide sources as there is unfortunately a great deal of rubbish on the web. One further tip: if you're looking for information on terrorism, bomb-making and other dubious activities, please *do* be careful what websites you visit. The men in black balaclavas who pay you a nocturnal visit and drag you away screaming may not heed your cries of 'I'm a writer'!

4. Active investigation

By active investigation I mean getting out there and getting a taste of what you're writing about, if you lack prior experience. One of my students wanted to write a thriller about racing drivers. Her storyline and character ideas were great, but conscious that her knowledge of Formula 1 motorsport was limited she started frequenting the Silverstone racing circuit. This is a great way of being able to put a real feel into your book – the sights, the sounds, the smells, the quintessence of a place or an activity.

Know your setting

Get familiar with your locations, if you aren't already. Many writers set their stories where they live, and all sorts of locations can be effective – from a remote rural village to the heart of a big city. The obvious advantage with setting your story on home ground is that you'll know it well and be able to convey it vividly to the reader. However, many thrillers also employ a variety of exotic locations that writers may not be so familiar with. These need to be reasonably accurately depicted: remember that today's readers are considerably better travelled than they were even just 20 years ago. Many of your future readers may recognise the errors in your description of, say, Paris or Rome – and although it matters not one jot in terms of how exciting or thrilling your book is, it will hurt to have your crimes gleefully exposed on the Amazon.com book reviews.

If you want to include one or more exotic locations in your thriller, and you can't actually go there to carry out your research, arm yourself with holiday brochures, tourist guides and maps. Many tourism websites now offer virtual tours online, which are a good way of getting the feel and layout of a place without having to spend a fortune getting there. Casually slipping a few local sights, restaurants, street names, etc., will help to create an authentic feel to the setting. If your story involves dramatic incidents such as blowing up buildings, you may wish to create an original setting based on real-life places. You can't really blow up the Vatican, for instance! (Though you can get a lot of exciting mileage out of *threatening* to blow it up, as Dan Brown does in *Angels and Demons.*)

More remote and inhospitable places – deserts, jungles, wildernesses – can be researched from travel books, accounts written by explorers and mountaineers, etc., as well as watching movies that have been filmed there (e.g. *Tears of the Sun* for the African jungle, *Proof of Life* for South America). You can afford to use a little more imagination in redesigning such locations, as it's unlikely that your reader will know better.

But don't get *too* hung up on research!

To balance out the above, I would urge you never to forget that you're writing a *thriller*. Your primary aim is to thrill and entertain, not to regurgitate a police procedure manual or firearms drill, or teach a history or geography lesson. It's all a question of balance: too *few* details, or wrong details, may make your story unconvincing, but too *many* details will bore the reader. Make it authentic enough to lull modern-day audiences into a state of suspended disbelief . . . and then, once that's in place and the scene is set, it's time to lay reality aside and concentrate on telling your story.

Likewise, if using travel guides for research, don't be tempted to turn your writing into a guidebook in its own right by throwing too many details at the reader. Readers don't need to know what the Eiffel tower looks like, or what year such-and-such memorial was built, or which way the leaning tower of Pisa leans (unless you're going to have one of your baddies chucked off the top of it and it's important to the plot!).

KILLER TITLES

A powerful asset for any thriller is its title. Imagine your title embossed in monolithic gold letters on the cover. It should be catchy, punchy, and not too long – two or three words is the optimum. The title's main function is to reach out and grab the reader's attention as they browse through the bookstore, website or catalogue. Make it as hard-hitting as you can.

Some good titles are (in my opinion):

◆ *Bolt*
◆ *Borrowed Time*
◆ *Die Trying*
◆ *Digital Fortress*
◆ *Oblivion*
◆ *One Shot*
◆ *Out of Sight*
◆ *The Eighth Day*
◆ *The First Horseman*
◆ *The Genesis Code*

These titles are all commanding, muscular and eye-catching. Some give an impression of what the story may involve, e.g. *Borrowed Time*, while others are more obscure, e.g. *Oblivion*. Some have a brutal quality that seem to grab you by the collar and force you to pick them up, e.g. *Bolt*, *One Shot*. And the last three, *The First Horseman*, *The Eighth Day* and *The Genesis Code*, all have that compelling and somehow ennobled biblical feel about them: it's always good to have a browse through the Bible to trawl for new ideas . . . though beware of worn-out clichés, as this is a well-trodden path already.

The right title
Don't worry too much if that perfect title doesn't come to you immediately. Think up a decent working title as a stop-gap. A better one may come to you in the course of writing –

sometimes part of a phrase may leap out at you screaming 'use me!'. For instance, somewhere in Lee Child's thriller *Die Trying* is the line 'Jack Reacher will save her, or he'll die trying'. You can just hear the writer thinking 'oho, that'll make a nice title'.

Sometimes the title doesn't have to relate directly to the storyline or even the characters. In another of the same author's thrillers, *Persuader*, the reader only learns late on what the title refers to, and it turns out to be only a passing detail (although I won't give it away here!). Nonetheless, *Persuader* perfectly evokes the hard-hitting tone of the novel.

Avoid the obvious

A writer friend came up with a sizzling idea for a neo-Nazi conspiracy thriller and wanted to call it *The Fourth Reich*. I strongly suspected that a search of Amazon.com would reveal that someone else had beaten him to it – in fact there were seven or eight writers who'd already used that title or ones very close to it. While there's no copyright on titles and in principle authors are fairly free to pick what they like, some ideas are really just a bit *too* obvious.

GETTING INTO TROUBLE

Libel

Nothing will shoot your project down in flames faster than the shadow of libel. No publisher will touch your story if there is any risk of a real-life figure, especially a powerful and well-connected one, sending their lawyers round.

Real-life people can often provide inspiration for a great villain, but be absolutely certain that you've put enough distance between the model and the fictitious character, especially if you're planning to have them commit all kinds of monstrous actions. Likewise, do make sure that none of your characters, especially the corrupt, crooked or otherwise morally dubious ones, have names that could identify them with any real-life person of similar occupation. (So forget about Terry Blair and Gerald Bush, for a start.)

Guarding against plagiarism

Let's face it, no story is entirely original. Most plots are variations on themes that have been visited many times, and you can often sum up a storyline in terms of its influences: X meets Y with a sprinkling of Z. In this slightly incestuous environment writers can occasionally feel tempted to 'pay tribute' to their favourite thrillers by incorporating ideas from them into their own.

However, do *please* make sure – as far as you can – that your chosen plot hasn't already been done by someone else. There's only thing worse than investing a load of time and effort into a project only to be told by a friend '*hey, doesn't that sound a bit like such-and-such?*' – that's for the book to proceed as far as publication only to land you in court! Even accidental plagiarism, however innocent, can get you into trouble. Publishers cover themselves by requiring the author to sign a statement, as part of their contract, that their work is original. However, they won't forgive you if they think you've tried to pull a fast one.

'Has anyone beaten me to it?' Checking for originality
Checking the originality of your story is much, much easier nowadays than it used to be. Use the internet search engines as your sniffer-dog, entering key phrases, titles and anything else that may reveal that your great idea is less original than you hoped. Alternatively, an hour spent browsing through the bookstore can tell you what you want to know.

Don't become too fixated on trying to achieve complete originality, however. I recently picked up a new bestselling title by a big-name author whose plot centres around an amnesiac ex-special forces soldier who wakes up one day with a bullet in him, wondering who he is and what his past was . . . now, doesn't that sound just a little like Robert Ludlum's *The Bourne Identity*?

Once you've assured yourself that your thriller idea is acceptably original and you're not treading on anyone's toes, all you have to do now is write it and get it published quickly before someone else gets the idea!

Workshop for Chapter 2

Choose a topic you're unfamiliar with, for instance:

➤ Doctors struggling to contain a deadly virus.

➤ The fight against wildlife poaching in Africa.

➢ How you would go about breaking into a secure building, e.g. a lab or an art gallery.

Or is there anything else that attracts you? Do some research and write a 200-word or more account to summarise what you've learned.

➢ Refer back to the heading 'Some tough questions!' in Chapter 2. Choose a thriller novel and imagine yourself as its author, just starting out and developing the story. Imagine how that writer would have answered those tough questions – why was the story worth writing? What made it appealing to a publisher? How was it different from others in its class? What did the writer bring to the deal that he or she alone was able to do? Jot down your ideas and keep them as a reference for when you answer them about your own thriller project.

(3)

The Plot

So now you have your basic idea. Next comes the fun part of crafting it into a plot, where inspiration gives way to perspiration and you begin to hammer the raw elements into shape.

THE ANATOMY OF A THRILLER

Think of a thriller as a living organism, a complex structure of organs and tissues all working together in harmony. That structure all hangs on a framework we call a skeleton, which gives it shape and rigidity and without which it would just fall in a slushy heap. In turn, all the peripheral bits of the skeleton, the arms and legs and tail if it has one, all hang on a central structure that runs through the body and connects everything together – the backbone. When we describe someone lacking courage and integrity as 'spineless', we're acknowledging the fact that without a spine, we are nothing! A thriller is just the same.

The backbone of the story

Just like every skeleton needs a backbone, every good plot needs to have a single line running through it that holds it together. Some of the best thrillers have a very simple plot-line, so that if you were describing it to a friend you could do it in a nutshell. For instance, the backbone of *The Fulcanelli Manuscript*, for all its convolutions and intertwined sub-plots, is simply that the hero is asked to find a mysterious cure for a sick child and sets out to track it down. The thriller *Absolute Power* is similarly held together by a very simple basic plotline: a jewel thief raiding a luxury house witnesses a killing in which the US President is implicated. When the killers discover that someone knows their secret, they launch a manhunt against him.

Of course, the few words you can fit into a nutshell doth not a full-length novel make. There has to be a lot more to it – but whatever happens, that central line, the story's back-bone, must always be clearly visible throughout. Don't let the reader lose sight of it. You can have as many sub-plots as you like (or as many as the story will accommodate), as long as you don't start allowing these to obscure or hinder the central line. If you do, the reader is liable to get confused, bored, and give up.

The main sub-plot of *Absolute Power*, for example, is the relationship between the thief and his daughter, which gives depth to the characters. She is a lawyer, and has never approved of her father's criminal ways. But his love for her and his desire to protect her are the redeeming features that make the audience empathise with a career criminal, and also make father and daughter come closer together as the story progresses. The fact that the baddies come after the daughter creates more tension and excitement, and the flirtatious relationship between her and the cop who's also chasing her father brings yet more depth and interest.

But interesting as they may be, these sub-plots would amount to little if you took away the backbone of the story: the underlying fact that the thief has information that could bring down the President. First and foremost, the story is about him and what he witnessed, and whether or not he's going to survive the experience. How's he going to get out of trouble? Will the dark forces of corrupt government get him and manage to suppress the awful truth? This is the power-house of the story, from where all its energy comes. Family business, personal themes, romantic elements, character development, all come later. They are the icing, not the cake.

Building it up from the middle

The best way to construct a plot is to start with the nucleus, the central line, or the backbone. Say, for instance, the central idea is 'terrorists hijack aeroplane with 400 people on board'. This has promise – it has natural tension, plays on people's fears of flying (and being blown up), and is a good reliable sort of thriller storyline – but it's still only a thin idea.

So you start to build it up, working outwards as you build up the layers. You need a goodie. Who's it to be? Say you opt to have a crack team of commandos smuggled on board. Sounds good? Now what? They need to figure out how to overcome the terrorists and land the plane safely. Just one problem: it turns out there's a giant bomb on board and enough nerve gas to wipe out half the eastern seaboard of the United States – which, we realise, is the terrorists' real intention. A million twists and turns later, we manage to defuse the bomb, kill the baddies and reclaim control of the plane. Phew!

You may have recognised the above as the storyline of the excellent thriller movie, *Executive Decision*. What really makes this a superlative story is its absolute simplicity. Even though it abounds with detail and a new twist comes up about every half-minute to wrack our nerves even more, we never lose sight of that clear line running through it. If you can construct a story with that kind of elegant, awesome beauty and execute it with skill, you will have a potential bestseller on your hands.

Weave the sub-plots smoothly through and around the main storyline. Introducing a sub-plot, then resolving it too soon, tends to kill tension and create a choppy rhythm and an episodic feel to the story.

STORYBOARDING

This term is borrowed from film-making, and I use it to describe the process of building up the key points of a plot, from initial ideas to fully-developed storyline. Many film-makers create a shot-by-shot series of hundreds of cartoon-like sketches to help them get the scenes fixed in their minds before shooting. Writers can do the same within their imagination, helping to visualise each scene clearly before it's written. Instead of pictures, a writer can create a flowing series of short paragraphs describing each scene or 'shot' in turn. These paragraphs may develop from just a single short line, a tiny idea, or a phrase of dialogue.

The computer is the ideal tool for building up your story-board, allowing you to 'inject' new material and ideas at the right points, and to move things around to get the best flow.

Your first storyboarded sketch of the plot, which might be on a document simply titled 'Book idea', could look something like this:

Conspiracy Theory Thriller

◆ Innocent hero stumbles on a top-level government plot.

◆ Remote Scottish village to be used as a testing-ground for fiendish weapon.

◆ Ensuing devastation whitewashed in media as a freak natural disaster.

Here you have the makings of an interesting idea, but it's full of holes and we have little idea of who the main character is. As it starts to take shape, details begin to get fleshed out:

◆ Innocent hero (who is he? Bruce McAra, investigative journalist) arrives in a remote Scottish village (why? for a three-day camping/birdwatching break – girlfriend has just left him, he needs some time to think and get away from it all).

◆ Out at night, he discovers something suspicious (chance meeting with teenage boy, who tells him that weird things are happening in the area).

- Military trucks are moving at night. What are they carrying?

- Bruce finds a disused military base a few miles from the village. But it's not as disused as it seems. More mysterious night convoys. What's going on?

- Start introducing other villagers.

- Funeral – someone has died under odd circumstances.

- Bruce witnesses something, gets chased and nearly caught.

- Awful realisation.

- The horror begins.

It's still full of holes, but now it's beginning to look like a story! As you continue to flesh it out, you'll see the setting coming to life as the villagers adopt names and personalities. Bruce will probably find a love interest in the shape of some attractive girl. We'll gain a better sense of Bruce's character and back-story. And through it all, the horrible truth of the conspiracy will begin to unfold, and the characters will find themselves caught up in a very dangerous situation. Not all will survive. Then, somehow, the story has to resolve itself.

As you add more and more bulleted points and these paragraphs swell and multiply, chapters will begin to emerge from the morass. You can move back and forth along the 'spine', adding bits here and there, or moving things from place to place. For instance, in this story it's important for the boy to have some skill with a crossbow (for later use), and so a scene can be inserted early on showing him hunting a couple of rabbits for his mother to put in a stew. He also sells them to the local butcher, allowing us to introduce that character for later use. (At the same time, this is giving a sense of what rural life might be like in the far north of Scotland, and painting a picture of a living community.)

And so on and so forth, until the story has finally started to grow into a book. Sooner or later, you will have actually started to *write* it, or bits of it, and these bits will sit alongside notes and ideas for a long time like a finished house in a half-built street. Don't despair if it looks messy and chaotic at this stage – building sites usually do, but there's method to the madness. The main thing is to get the ideas down.

To help sort through what may look like a terrible muddle, you might want to try a colour-coding system such as the one I use:

◆ RED for wild ideas or half-baked notions that come to you suddenly and may or may not work.

◆ BLUE for semi-developed plot points that will probably be kept, but may be changed or moved around.

◆ BLACK ('automatic') for things you're happier with, that are more fully fleshed out and need only minor revision.

PLANTING SEEDS

A 'seed' in a storyline can be many things: it's the carving knife somebody left on the table; the car keys somebody forgot to take out of the ignition; the faulty door latch that they never got around to fixing; that undeveloped camera film; the unread note in the dead man's fist; the address book slipped in a breast pocket that will later turn a .38 slug; the mysterious phone call somebody made although we don't yet know what was said; the tiniest clue buried in a heap of dialogue.

This is also known as *foreshadowing*. When such a detail is discreetly, offhandedly planted early on in the story, it may seem very minor and inconsequential. But it can – indeed it *should*, to justify its existence at all – go on to play a very important part later on in the story. Sometimes it provides clues for the hero to go on, and sometimes it saves their life.

If you study the best plots (either book or film) you'll see that nothing is ever wasted and ALL 'seeds' will later grow into important aspects of the plot. Well handled, this can seem to the reader or viewer as sheer genius! Little does the audience suspect how much work may have gone into putting the plot together.

Working backwards

A lot of literary seed-planting involves a process of working backwards, retrospectively introducing elements that will become important later on. Say you come to a point in the development of the plotline where a character is in trouble and you can't think of a way to get them out. Well, how about we go back to some convenient point of the plot and plant a discreet little seed?

Like the boy with the crossbow above, it could be a simple detail, a short scene, that later provides a believable escape-route: our hero Bruce is cornered by a baddie, and the boy comes in and saves him by putting a crossbow bolt in the attacker. The reader will have no problem believing this could happen, since they've already seen how good the kid was at shooting rabbits. Thus the story starts to work fluidly as a whole, and nobody will ever know that this handy little marksman was only added in as an afterthought!

As you go on planting more seeds and creating a whole seamless network of links through the story, you can devise a plot that's as tight as a drum, highly effective and believable. The reader takes in a story from A to Z, but the writer works in a zig-zag, always moving back and forth, spinning the story like a spider's web.

USING A MINOR CHARACTER

Quite often, a minor character can be drafted in out of the blue (as opposed to seeded in earlier) to help heroes out of sticky situations, provide crucial information, and introduce major new plot elements. At one point in *The Da Vinci Code*, our heroes are caught in a seemingly impossible situation as police surround the bank where they're trying to access vital information. Enter André Vernet, the bank manager, who kindly helps them to escape. In another Dan Brown novel, *Angels and Demons*, a convenient tour guide innocently provides the hero with crucial information to help his search. Even a minor character with a brief walk-on part can have a big impact on the story. But don't rely on this device too often, or it will seem like there's a handy contrived character lurking behind every piece of scenery, ready to pop out with a placard reading 'BIG CLUE HERE' or 'STEP THIS WAY FOR EASY ESCAPE'.

'I'D FORGOTTEN HIM': KEEPING THE BALLS IN THE AIR

In a story with quite a few characters and settings, you need to make sure that your reader always knows what's going on and never forgets who a character is or what they're doing in the story. At a certain point in the writing of *The Fulcanelli Manuscript*, my agent prompted me with the words 'I'd forgotten him!'. As the story grew and swelled, I'd allowed too many pages to go by in-between mentions of a minor character who would later become an important element of the story. There was a risk that anyone reading it would lose that thread and later get confused when the character re-emerged.

Having identified this problem, it was then a fairly simple matter of inserting a small scene or two to keep the reader's awareness of the character alive while other elements of the story were playing out. Because the novel was written in the authorial mode where the 'camera' is the 'all-seeing eye' and able to flit from scene to scene and character to character unhindered by the constraints of a viewpoint, it was an easy fix.

KEEPING SUB-PLOTS 'ON THE BOIL'

A similar problem can arise with sub-plots. If a sub-plot is introduced at a certain point in the story and then left untouched for a long time while the main storyline and other sub-plots are moving forwards, the reader could forget and lose the thread.

This problem happened to director Tony Scott in the making of the film *Spy Game*. The story centres on the attempts of a CIA agent (Robert Redford) to rescue a friend and former colleague (Brad Pitt) from a Chinese prison. Through a mixed series of flashbacks and present-day scenes we piece together a picture of the relationship between these two men, the loyalty and the friction between them. As the complex story unfolded in the editing-room, Tony Scott began to realise that he was in danger of letting the audience forget the urgent predicament that the Pitt character was in by focusing too much on flashbacks and intrigue. His solution to the problem was to call Brad Pitt back in for re-shoots to allow him to insert some new short scenes reminding us that while everything else is going on, poor old Brad is being beaten up in a prison. This kept the story tight and maintained a sense of urgency.

So when putting together your story, just like making a movie, be aware of what all the elements of the plot are doing at any given moment, and don't let more than a certain time period (say 50 pages) go by without recapping on any plot elements lest they become dormant. It's like stoking a fire with a poker, injecting oxygen into dying coals to get them burning again.

Another way to see it is as a juggling act: you need to keep all your balls in the air, all the time. Incidentally, if you are still writing without a computer, this kind of insertion will be much harder to do: it's one of those times when the flexibility afforded by the machine actually becomes an integral part of the writing process.

HOW CHARACTERS DICTATE PLOT

Your plot will be a living and evolving thing that may keep changing right until the end of the writing process. Part of what makes the plot evolve is your developing relationship with your main characters, especially the hero or heroine. As you get to know them and develop them better, giving them more and more depth of character, this may have an effect on the plot. Plot and character are very interdependent, and we'll focus on character in the next chapter.

CONTINUITY

Keeping the overview
As your story begins to take shape, it will start to grow into a hefty chunk of words – bearing in mind that the finished item could be anywhere between 100,000–175,000 words, maybe even more. Like a large land mass whose boundaries are too big to patrol effectively, it becomes increasingly difficult to keep an overview of the entire thing.

One problem that can arise from this is continuity, or the lack of it. This is especially the case if you've been moving blocks of text around in an attempt to find the best flow, and even more likely to happen if you're dealing with a complex plot that evolves and changes as you develop it. Continuity is simply making sure that if Sally was wearing a green anorak with a ripped left sleeve on page 80, it hasn't magically mutated into a blue one with a ripped right sleeve by page 150. Or, worse, that the dead man the police inspector is referring to on page 200 won't actually be found shot in the woods until page 250! Believe it or not, these oversights can, and do, happen.

Using the computer as a continuity aid

In the 'bad old days' before computers, it could be hard for writers to keep a check on continuity – even the great French novelist, Gustave Flaubert, keeps changing the colour of his Madame Bovary's eyes! But now there's no excuse. Use the search facility on your machine (usually denoted by a little pair of binoculars) to search for keywords: names or other words that will enable you to scan quickly through the text and hunt down any anomalies before some embarrassing incident occurs. You don't want the prospective agent or publisher to be the first to find these errors.

LOOKING AHEAD TO SEQUELS

It's not necessarily too presumptuous for the first-time thriller author to be thinking ahead to a time when their first book is out there and readers want more. Is there enough meat on your idea to keep it going for ten novels without running thin? Do you know enough about your genre/ background?

The franchise-worthy character

Many of today's most successful thriller writers have built their career on a single character with enough appeal to sustain a whole series of novels. A writer who can think up a character with 'legs' enough for a successful franchise could be sitting on a potential goldmine. The obvious benefits (other than the money) are that you don't have to dream up a whole new hero with each new story, and your knowledge of the character will be so intimate that he/she will become very real to your loyal and growing band of readers. Each successive novel in a successful series helps to sell more of the others.

So, if you think you may have created a lead character full of commercial promise – a Jack Reacher, Nick Stone or Robert Langdon – it may be unwise to finish Episode 1 with them unavailable for a sequel: such as dead, crippled or married (all of which would be equally limiting to such heroes' prospects). *Do* make sure that your story is a closed loop in its own right, with all loose ends tied up and no obvious 'I'll be back'-type references, as this is sure to put publishers off very quickly. But don't be too eager to let your sensational lead character die a heroic death, because if there is real quality in your work you may well find yourself, a year or two hence, bringing that character back for the next round.

Workshop for Chapter 3

➢ Read a thriller and make structural analysis notes on its plot. Identify the central line that runs through it. Observe how the sub-plots work around it – where do they first emerge and how are they introduced? How do they tie into the main plot, and how are they resolved? Apply these ideas to your own story. Would any of them work?

➢ While reading, keep an eye open for planted 'seeds', or pieces of information that foreshadow later events. Make note of them, observing how the writer makes use of them. Could you have thought of a better way?

➢ If you haven't already done so, begin to lay out your own thriller plot in 'storyboarded' form. Start off with simple ideas, and don't be afraid to experiment. See how changing the sequence of scenes and events around affects the story, and focus on finding the most effective structure.

(4)

Character

The core of your thriller is, or should be, its characters. Strong, engaging characters are what will make the story work – without them, even the most sensational and twisty plotline is powerless.

THE CHARACTER-DRIVEN PLOT

In real life, barring earthquakes, volcanic eruptions and acts of God, it's *people* who make things happen. Wars are started as a result of human psychology: hatred, greed, the lust for power. Human conflicts at all levels are generated and fuelled by human wants and desires, human problems and failings. The virtues and vices that are forever locked in a struggle of good and evil all come not from some abstract source, but from us.

In a story, then, it's the characters who should be making things happen, driving the plot. A story where characters seem to just meander along 'following the script', will be weak and lifeless, and the characters themselves will seem wooden and unreal. A powerful and thrilling read is one where the character psychology provides the motivation for people's behaviour: for instance, the man who takes on the risky job to clear his name or purge the guilt he suffers from some past mistake; or a person's struggle to do the right thing in the face of terrible adversity. A great deal of raw emotional power can be created by showing how characters cope with their challenges, how they suffer, the moral dilemmas they face, the desperate things they may have to do, and perhaps how badly they want to escape from the responsibility that's been placed on them. These are the things that will make your characters seem real to the reader.

CREATING REAL CHARACTERS

If your reader can't identify with your main characters, why should they care what happens to them? The moment it occurs to them that, really, they don't *feel* one way or the other if the hero gets shot, or his car gets hit by the train, they will lose their incentive to read on and you've lost them.

Readers are far more likely to identify with a 'real' person, who has all the flaws and weaknesses that we recognise in ourselves, and the virtues and strengths that we'd all like to have. Make your characters as three-dimensional as you can, and get to know them better than you know your friends and family. In fact, you should get to know them so well that when you stop writing, you will acutely miss their company. If you can get to the point where you catch yourself thinking 'no, my character wouldn't say that/wouldn't act that way', it's a good sign.

Avoid clichés

The 'strong, silent type', the slinky femme fatale and the cackling villain are among the many stereotypes of yesteryear that are either dead already or fast heading for the knacker's yard. Even the venerable James Bond is running into trouble in the twenty-first century, and in a bid to keep the franchise alive his producers are working hard to do away with the 'Mr Perfect' image and to re-invent him as a more fallible and accessible character.

Luc Simon: evolution of a character

Inspector Luc Simon, one of the main characters in my thriller *The Fulcanelli Manuscript*, started life as a minor character with little more than a walk-on part and a completely different name. Here's how he looked in his first incarnation (to set the scene for you, the location is Paris, and the heroine has just reported a murder; the cops come to investigate):

> A team of police officers arrived just as she was pulling up outside her building. They were headed by a tall, burly, plain-clothes man wearing a brown leather jacket and smoking a pipe. A large moustache covered virtually his whole mouth, giving him a walrus-like appearance. The look on his face was that of a man who has seen everything, for whom nothing can come as a surprise. 'I am Inspecteur Delavigne,' he said in a gruff voice.

Out of this rather too obvious and stereotyped Clouseau-like character, a whole new character evolved during the next draft of the novel. First to go were the pipe and the moustache. He became a younger man, more intense, ambitious and obsessive, addicted to coffee as the only thing that could relieve his stress-related headaches. As his character evolved, I found myself wanting to give him more to do, and by the final draft he was playing a very major role. I realised that the reader should meet him earlier in the plot, and I did this by creating a whole new back-story for him, with a marriage heading for the rocks due to the demands of his job and his single-minded devotion to it. Not only did this serve to make him seem more real, but the stress of his personal life also gave depth to some of his behaviour – his impatience, his tough treatment of the heroine, his general state of emotional tension. By creating a difficult personal life for this character, it became possible for the reader to empathise with him and forgive some of his mistakes and his occasional unpleasantness.

So, out of a one-dimensional cartoon character grew a man about whom I could talk for a long time as though describing a real friend – someone with troubles, someone who could feel pain as well as joy.

Aim to build your characters up in the same kind of way. It doesn't really matter if in the planning stages, or even in the first draft, they come over as a little wooden and under-developed. By the time you've lived with them for a while, you'll begin to form an idea of what direction they could grow in, and how to breathe life into them. As you move closer to the final draft, you'll have them jumping off the page.

Beware of the biography

The worst thing you can do with your character is to blurt out his or her life story and entire background when the reader first meets them. Let's take the above example of Inspector Luc Simon, the Parisian cop with the troubled home life. How would the following strike you as an introduction to the character?

> Luc Simon was furious as he walked up the steps to the police headquarters, where he'd worked for the last ten years. He hadn't felt like coming into work at all today, after his sleepless night. His wife Hélène had announced over dinner that she was leaving him for another guy. She'd said she couldn't stand living with a workaholic who never paid her any attention.
>
> Maybe she was right, he thought, and reflected on all the failed relationships in his life. Ever since he'd been a small boy he'd always dreamed of being a cop. It was all that had ever mattered to him.

Isn't that just excruciating? It's flat and uninteresting, and will probably make the readers think they'd have left him too. It fails to bring the character to life. This passage is screaming information like a man under torture – there's no doubt that by the end of it we know quite a lot about the character – but nothing that makes him seem real, interesting or appealing.

Show and tell

The rule is that you don't *tell* such details to the reader: you *show* them.

Luc Simon was running late. He'd changed into his smart suit at the police headquarters, running to the car still tying his tie as his officers wondered where the inspector was dashing off to all dressed up.

He checked his watch as he skidded through the Paris traffic. He'd booked the table at Guy Savoy for eight. It was 8.33 p.m. when he got there. A waiter ushered him across the room. The restaurant was full of diners and a buzz of conversation. Soft jazz played in the background. He could see Hélène sitting at the table for two in the corner, her glossy black hair obscuring her face as she flipped tensely through a magazine. He asked the waiter to bring champagne right away, and went to join her.

'Let me guess,' she sighed as he sat down opposite her at the small round table. 'You couldn't get away.'

'I got here as fast as I could. Something came up.'

'As usual. Even on your wedding anniversary, work comes first, doesn't it.'

'Well, this is the thing. Homicidal maniacs don't generally have a lot of respect for people's personal schedules,' he muttered, feeling that familiar barrier of tension rising up fast between them. That was pretty usual, too. 'Ah, here's the champagne,' he said, trying his best to smile.

What have we learned from this scene so far? That Luc Simon is a busy police inspector who's always in a tearing hurry. He's practical in his ways – look how he took his suit to work knowing he wouldn't have time to go home to change. We've also learned that Luc is a homicide cop who deals with a lot of ugly crime, and devotes much of his time to his job. He's married to Hélène, and it's their anniversary. However, things are not going well, and despite the fancy restaurant and the champagne there is a frosty atmosphere between them. (In fact, Hélène is just about to break the news that she's leaving him for another man.) But you can see that he's trying to make things work out, doing his best to juggle his personal life and career. He's a living human being with problems, just like you and me.

In other words, by showing a slice of Luc's life to the reader instead of just rattling off the facts about it, we can convey a far greater depth of information.

Likewise, if you want to portray your main character as someone extremely courageous, don't *say* they are – show the reader something to make them see it for themselves. Consider the following two lines:

◆ Mrs Brown was a brave and selfless woman.

◆ Mrs Brown ran into a burning building to rescue a trapped child.

Line 1 is telling us something important about Mrs Brown, but as an attempt to convey her character it's lifeless. Line 2 is essentially giving us exactly the same information, but now we can really *feel* just how brave she is, and we can visualise her going in through the flames and the heat, choking on the black smoke, then emerging with the child safe in her arms. Line 2 makes no attempt to praise Mrs Brown for what she has done, or to put words in the reader's mouth. It leaves the reader to judge her by her actions, and thus engages them emotionally. Result: an infinitely more powerful line of writing.

Apply this rule with all characters. Don't *tell* me the guy is bad; *show* me. Don't *tell* me the other guy feels guilty about something he's done in the past; *show* him slugging back the scotch to help him forget, and haunted at night by terrible nightmares. If you can keep it a mystery why he's so tormented, the reader will want to know more. Then, on page 250, the character can finally crack and spill his terrible secret, perhaps in the form of a confession to someone. Build up emotional tension, and characters will come to life.

There are various ways that you can show the character's qualities to the reader without seeming to spell them out. In *The Da Vinci Code*, Dan Brown uses a particular device to reveal some background information about his hero, Robert Langdon. Langdon, an academic, is just about to give a talk at a conference. The hostess introducing him to the audience jokily reads out what a magazine has written about him: that he'd been nominated as one of Boston's top ten intriguing people; that he was known for his captivating presence and his low baritone voice that was described by his admiring female students as 'chocolate for the ears'. The magazine has gone on to depict him as 'Harrison Ford in Harris tweed'. Langdon's reaction to this introduction is to squirm with embarrassment. When he stands up to give his speech his humorous opening line is 'Boston magazine clearly has a gift for fiction . . . and if I find out which one of you provided that article I'll have the Consulate deport you'.

Through this device, we've learned lots about Langdon in just a couple of paragraphs: that he's attractive and fit, highly regarded, well-dressed, witty and self-effacing. Readers are being discreetly invited to 'cast' him in their minds as Harrison Ford. Because Harrison Ford is synonymous in the reader's mind with his famous swashbuckling Indiana Jones film role, *without needing to be told* we now have a subtle impression of Langdon as a capable action hero as well as an erudite professor. All this information is conveyed within the first three pages of meeting Langdon, and never once do we feel it's being rammed down our throats.

Put your character through the mill

Real human beings suffer pain, become scared, have doubts, get out of their depth. And so should your characters, if they are to seem to the reader like 'one of us' and not some impossibly capable and remote character who strolls through the story without any worries. At a certain stage in your plot, the hero/heroine should really be having a tough time psychologically or physically, or both. If things are too easy for them, or if they're allowed to be too happy for too long, the reader will start to get bored.

Showing how your characters respond under great pressure is also the ultimate way to reveal their true nature. As in real life, it's when things get tough that the cracks will show, cowardly or selfish tendencies come out, or else true heroism will prevail. A character who can endure harsh challenges and come through victorious is one who will win the admiration of the reader.

So make the character suffer a little – put up as many cruel obstacles as you can: deceptions and treachery, setbacks and disasters, blind alleys, traps, seemingly inescapable situations. The greater the suffering, the more heroic the ultimate triumph – as the saying goes, '*No Guts, No Glory*'. If you have done your job and made the reader empathise with your character, they will be tearing through the pages rooting for him and hoping he'll overcome the adversity you're slinging at him. For a cinematic example of how effective this can be, just watch the classic 80s thriller *Die Hard*, where heroic cop Bruce Willis gets progressively cut up, bruised and torn in his battle with the terrorist baddies.

Characters can be messed up . . .

One useful device is to afflict your main character with some kind of mild emotional or psychological 'issue'. This does two things:

1. It makes them seem more real and accessible and helps gain the reader's empathy.
2. It provides you with something to exploit for dramatic purposes.

The character might suffer from a phobia, for instance, like Robert Langdon's claustrophobia in *Da Vinci Code* or Indiana Jones's fear of snakes in *Raiders of the Lost Ark*. Skilled book or film writers don't build such features into their characters just for the sake of it – they deliberately plant them early in the story, while we're getting to know the character, and bring them back later to crank up the tension at some crucial moment. If the character has to confront their worst fears in order to win the day, that makes their heroism all the more complete.

Guilt, or shame over past actions, is another psychological feature often employed very effectively by writers. Robert Goddard is one thriller author who gives depth and drive to his characters by having them burdened by a shameful past (e.g. the teacher disgraced by his sordid escapades with the schoolgirl in *Past Caring*) or tormented by painful regrets (e.g. the hero's guilt about his wife's apparent suicide in *Sight Unseen*). Some characters are driven to the brink of despair by their inner demons and may have turned to drink as a result – Denzel Washington's character in the movie *Man on Fire* and Benedict Hope in *The Fulcanelli Manuscript* are two examples. Their guilt over past actions, and their quest for redemption, are what drives them and makes the story work on a human level.

. . . But not too messed up

However, don't make your characters too neurotic or damaged, or you risk alienating the reader. British readers will tend to become uncomfortable (more than their US cousins) if you have your characters in any kind of psychotherapy: they won't want to identify with them any more if they're 'mad'. Likewise, borderline alcoholics are acceptable but don't let your character descend into full-blown alcoholism or any sort of drug use if you want to keep your reader's empathy: it's just too squalid. Furthermore, someone who is permanently sloshed isn't going to be much use as a hero!

THE CHARACTER'S JOURNEY

In real life, people mature as they gain experience. They make mistakes, and sometimes have to pay the penalty for them emotionally and in other ways. But through that suffering they're often able to learn important life lessons, and hopefully become better people as a result. Perhaps our quest for self-betterment is the only thing that really gives meaning to our lives.

For a fictitious character to come across as real, their life should have something of the same learning curve or 'journey'. From the point where we first meet them to the point where we leave them, they should have changed in some way. Maybe they've learned something about themselves, overcome their weaknesses, stood up and triumphed over adversity, found it in themselves to love. Whatever their development arc, the person we find on page 1 shouldn't be the same person we wave goodbye to at the end of the book.

Any time you come across a book or film character who lacks depth or seems wooden, you'll find it's at least partly because the writer didn't take them on that journey. They stay the same throughout the story, learn nothing, and fail to engage us emotionally.

SOME BASIC CHARACTER TYPES

Thriller characters can come in all shapes and sizes, but all the main characters in successful thrillers have one thing in common: their ability to make the reader relate to them in some way.

The loser who transcends himself

The 'loser' is the character whose life hasn't gone according to plan. Often without any prospects or money, they may have been abandoned by their spouse and/or be facing eviction from their apartment, had their car repossessed, etc. That doesn't mean they're completely useless as people – they might often be well educated and well qualified for something, such as Martin Radford, the out-of-work historian in Robert Goddard's *Past Caring*, or the struggling artist Danny Cray in John Case's *The Eighth Day*. It's just that they've never got their act together or made much of themselves. Until, that is, they become embroiled in the intrigue of the thriller! Through whatever unexpected challenges that come their way, these characters discover or rediscover qualities in themselves that have lain dormant; they come alive again, transcend themselves and win the day against the odds. The story ends with them looking at a brighter new future, even though they may have suffered to get there.

Why do readers identify with this character? Well, don't we see part of that character in ourselves? We all feel that we could better ourselves, seize the day a bit more, take a chance to prove to ourselves and others that we *can* win. Yes, dammit! The loser who throws off his self-imposed shackles is a powerful archetype.

The hero who is talented but must overcome his demons to succeed

The flawed hero, like the loser, has negative inner qualities that drag him down. Where he differs from the loser is that he's excellent at what he does. He may be a very driven person, but what drives him to be great may also be what haunts him and weakens him. This character often has a bad past, perhaps a traumatic incident that happened long ago, perhaps a source of terrible guilt, some secret that is to be revealed in the course of the story. One such character is Ben Hope in *The Fulcanelli Manuscript*: in his professional life he's the best, but as a human being he's a lost soul and a borderline alcoholic. This character, and his story arc, is the age-old tale of redemption.

Why will the reader empathise? Many of us feel guilty about things in the past, or have other demons and weaknesses that we would like to cleanse out. When we see these in our hero, we'll understand him deeply on a human level, and as he strives to transcend his problems, we are with him all the way and feel inspired by his example.

The hero who's a little out of his depth

I can't think of a better recent example than Robert Langdon from *The Da Vinci Code*. Langdon has many trappings of success – he's a professor, an intellectual, a hit with his female students. There's a touch of Indiana Jones about him in this respect. But while Indy is a superman outside the classroom, Langdon is slightly out of his element when being chased around by dark forces. He's the innocent victim, the fugitive, who stumbles around a little and has an eccentric tendency to stop and admire the architecture when the police are right on his heels!

Why do readers find him appealing? Although talented and gifted in many ways that the reader may not share, he is the Everyman who has been thrown in at the deep end. We look up at him for his erudition and brilliant mind, but when he's the innocent fugitive we feel equal to him, and we empathise.

The strong, silent type who is more than meets the eye

This is the character who sits smiling to himself in the corner of the bar-room while some big bully is strutting around intimidating people and showing everyone what a tough guy he is. The guy in the corner doesn't do or say anything – he's far too confident to need to prove himself – but we just know that if the bully should mess with him it'll be the last time he does. These heroes don't start fights . . . they just finish them. From Clint Eastwood to Steven Seagal, we've all seen this type of hero in a million movies. In the modern thriller, one of the best examples of him is Lee Child's creation Jack Reacher – former war hero-turned drifter.

In lesser hands, Jack Reacher might have become a cardboard cut-out, an unbelievable, anachronistic and inaccessible 'Mr Perfect'. But Lee Child cleverly avoids this by making Jack a very modest kind of guy. He has none of the smugness that has tended to affect James Bond, and he's never condescending in the way that Steven Seagal movie characters can be. He's a man of the people, happy to take modest jobs, never bragging too much about his abilities or his medals; a cool character who doesn't go looking for trouble . . . but when trouble finds him, as it invariably does, he knows how to deal with it. We feel in safe hands with Reacher – we never doubt his ability to win, but because he's a real person his adventures never become predictable.

Why do readers go for Reacher? According to the Daily Mail, 'Reacher is the sort of hero that no woman could help falling for'. Well, there you have it. Women apparently love him, and it therefore follows that men want to *be* him.

QUALITIES FOR A THRILLER HERO

Some desirable and undesirable qualities for your thriller hero or heroine:

DO make them:

◆ Tough and resilient

◆ Modest and generous

◆ Vulnerable and given to human faults

◆ Capable of transcending themselves

DON'T make them:

◆ Cruel or pitiless (the anti-hero went out with Dirty Harry Callahan)

◆ Cynical and greedy (unless this is set to change)

◆ Too flawed to be capable of redemption

◆ One-dimensionally perfect, infallible and always right

On sexy heroes and heroines

Make sure you understand what this means. A 'sexy' male hero is most emphatically not a womanising, lecherous, eyebrow-raising creep from the tired old James Bond school.

He is not the macho lover, and in fact a hero can be very sexy without ever even having sex with anyone; nor are strutting musclemen very appealing any more (if indeed they ever were). The term isn't meant, therefore, to be taken too literally.

By the same token, we shouldn't take the term 'sexy heroine' to mean a pneumatic blonde sporting Daisy Duke shorts and an intellect to match her astrology chart. What makes a heroine sexy, and what publishers want, is her strength, her determination, her smartness and independence of spirit.

We've come a long, long way from the misogynist dark ages when female thriller characters were all too often portrayed as silly fluffy things that would blubber hysterically for the least reason until a slap from a square-jawed, hairy-chested man brought them to their senses. In today's thriller the strong, smart, capable female character has, thankfully and rightfully, taken centre stage. One of the best of these is Deputy US Marshal Karen Sisco, the leading lady in Elmore Leonard's 1996 thriller *Out of Sight*, later played on the screen by Jennifer Lopez.

There's been a balancing out of the gender roles in recent years that has affected both sexes. Heroes and heroines are still tough and brave and admirable, but the spirit of the times (or what we'd like the spirit of the times to be) is reflected in the changing face of both. At one time we would never have seen the mighty Arnold Schwarzenegger play a defeated alcoholic – as we see him in the opening scenes of *End of Days*. The modern male hero is allowed to be weak, vulnerable, and flawed. While Mel Gibson weeps disconsolately in films like *Ransom*, *We Were Soldiers* and *Signs*, we see far less weepy emotionality in today's female leads, both in film and novel.

Don't pick at your food!

A note on character 'sexiness': a friend of mine who was writing a novel had created a male lead character who wasn't very interested in food, and tended to pick at it. This was done for a clear reason, to underline symbolically the character's (initial) lack of interest in life, his dark and depressed outlook. But when he gave it to female friends to read, they were unanimously repelled by the idea of a man who picks at his food! It was off-putting, they said. So the writer simply deleted the few lines where the character would leave his food half-eaten on the plate, and the problem seemed to be fixed. Sometimes, it's just the little things that can make a character unsexy!

FINDING THE RIGHT NAME FOR YOUR CHARACTER

Finding an effective and memorable name for a character can be a tricky business. Veteran thriller novelist, Elmore Leonard, is one of the great masters of the catchy name – Chilli Palmer (*Get Shorty*), Karen Sisco and Jack Foley (both from *Out of Sight*) all have that indefinable 'cool' that can be so hard to capture. American names in general, with their cosmopolitan blend of Irish, Italian, German, Polish, Jewish and other influences, often have a certain upbeat and exotic ring to them – especially to a British ear. However, don't rely on a cool name alone to make a character interesting. The strength has to come from within the character themselves.

Names don't have to be overblown or wildly unusual. More ordinary names such as Dr Tom Carter (*The Miracle Strain*), Tom Bishop (*Spy Game*), Harry Mitchell (*52 Pickup*), Harry Barnett (*Into the Blue*) and Andy McGee (*Firestarter*) can work well too. They're familiar to our ear, easy to identify with, and have a kind of earthy, meat-and-potatoes, family-man quality that encourages us to trust them. A name like this very much suits the 'ordinary guy thrown in at the deep end' scenario that is the core of many thrillers.

For some reason it's more fun thinking up great names for villains. You can often get away with slightly more theatrics for baddies. Foreign names like Maximilian Kohler (*Angels and Demons*) and Zerevan Zebek (*The Eighth Day*) sound suitably fiendish and create a nice contrast with more ordinary 'good guy' names such as those above.

Avoid using names that are too long-winded or hard to pronounce, especially for more prominent characters whose names the reader will have to read often. It's also important to avoid giving characters names that sound too similar to one another, lest the reader confuse them.

Other effective name ideas:

◆ Irish or Scottish names, e.g. Tom McAllister, Bruce McAra, Tara O'Sullivan, Brendan Casey, Terry Flynn.

◆ Alliteration in names, e.g. Zerevan Zebek (*The Eighth Day*), Gunther Glick, Vittoria Vetra (both from *Angels and Demons*), Munch Mancini (*An Unacceptable Death*), Roberta Ryder (*The Fulcanelli Manuscript*).

◆ Names with literary references, such as John Milton (the devil in Andrew Neiderman's supernatural thriller *The Devil's Advocate*).

Try to avoid jokey names – not even super-bestselling author, Dan Brown, should be allowed to get away with a name like Bishop Aringarosa (*The Da Vinci Code*). Not only does this sound like 'a ring of roses' from the children's nursery-rhyme, but in Italian 'aringarosa' translates literally as 'red herring'. And Leigh Teabing, another principal character in the same novel, is a scrambled and perhaps somewhat mischievous reference to the non-fiction authors Leigh and Baigent (spot the anagram?) who in 2005 took Dan Brown to court for plagiarism (and lost).

Find original names!

Someone who attended a writing class told me the following story: a group of writers were sitting together sharing bits of their work. A man who was new to the group was asked if he would like to read out some of what he'd brought, which he told them was a spy thriller he was working on. He started to read: '*Bond ran through the trees. He checked over his shoulder. He could hear the baying Dobermans in the distance. They were after him. He felt for his gun . . .*'

Before he got any further someone gently broke in and asked, as delicately as possible, 'Excuse me, did you just say "Bond"? That's your character's name? And this is a spy thriller?' 'Yes, it is,' replied the man, flushing a little. 'Why shouldn't I call him Bond? Bond's a perfectly good name, isn't it?' They pointed out to him, 'Well, you *are* aware that there's this other spy thriller character called Bond, who's been around for a long time and is, well, kind of famous?' At this, the man stood up, furiously proclaimed his undying *right* to call his characters anything he damn well pleased, cursed them all for a bunch of idiots and stormed out of the class never to be seen again.

Even if this 'Bond' thriller had been the most magnificent thing ever written, there isn't a publisher in the universe who would come within a light year of signing it up. Please, let's forget about our *rights* as artists and be sensible. It's really not that difficult to come up with a good name for a character . . . and there are many better names than Bond!

CRAMPING STYLE AND STEALING THUNDER

Avoid letting your character get swamped by another one. Lee Child makes a very smart move in his thriller *Die Trying*, in which tough hero Jack Reacher meets up, and finds himself sharing a hazardous situation with, sassy FBI agent Holly Johnson. She's a strong character, and she has to be – a normal civilian wouldn't be able to match Reacher or keep up with him as the book unfolds. But, given that she and Reacher spent a lot of the story together, there's the danger that she could be so capable – not to mention so sexy – that she could steal a little too much of Reacher's thunder. The author side-steps this potential problem by finding a means to weaken the Holly character: when we meet her she is on crutches with ligament damage from a sports accident, and for most of the story her mobility is badly affected by this injury. This means that she needs Reacher to protect her at crucial moments in the story, remaining a strong character in her own right, but allowing the main hero to stand out and be all the more heroic. It's a very simple idea, but a very effective one.

VILLAINS

Everybody loves a baddie. Without fiendish villains, there would be nothing to make heroes look heroic; in fact a thriller without a baddie would be like a crime novel with no crime, or a war story with no war. Villains are the source of all conflict, and conflict is the origin of every thriller. Whatever is happening in a thriller, it will invariably come down to the treachery, duplicity, greed, corruption and often murderous behaviour of one or more nasty characters.

Our relationship with such characters is paradoxical: on the one hand, we often find them highly seductive. They're often intelligent and capable, charming and sophisticated. We might sympathise with them to a degree, perhaps even agree with certain attitudes they express. But on the other hand, we're always pleased to witness their downfall. Seeing the baddie go down reaffirms the status quo and our sense of security.

If you think about it, we've been feeling this way about baddies ever since we were children listening to bedtime stories – once the monster or the wicked witch had been dealt with we could curl up and sleep soundly. The baddie is the bogeyman, the darkness, the terror that lurks in the wardrobe at night, everything that's bad and scary about the world. Once he's dead, the world is a safe place again.

The baddie as a tragic hero

Some baddies weren't born bad, but have for one reason or another gone down the wrong road. Like the tragic hero in classical literature – Shakespeare's Macbeth and Othello are men consumed with passions that destroy them – they might have a fatal character weakness that has allowed evil to take a hold and dictate their behaviour. Their character flaw can take various forms: a past experience that has rotted their heart, some kind of bitterness in their life that has sucked the good out of them, a mistaken belief that they're doing the right thing. While the thriller genre isn't necessarily the place to go delving deeply into the psychoanalytic profile of the flawed villain, you can nonetheless create very interesting baddies by giving the reader a sense of what makes them tick. That creates a human bond of empathy between the reader and the baddie that we may find somewhat unsettling; when the baddie is destroyed, the satisfaction we feel is partly from knowing that it's the dark side in ourselves that's been destroyed with him.

'Brain' baddies and 'brawn' baddies

In thrillers you often find that one 'brain' baddie, perhaps physically unmenacing but with a fiendish intellect, presides over a whole lot of 'brawn' baddies who are big and strong, but rather more dim-witted and generally expendable. The former is the mastermind who has the wicked plan and the intelligence to see it carried out, and the latter make this possible by means of their muscle. Michael Corleone is the brain baddie in *The Godfather*, and his gangsters in trench-coats and fedora hats are the brawn.

Often, the hero may have to deal with a few of the brawn baddies to get to the brain. Have plenty of expendable heavies handy, so that you can dispose of a few during the course of your story in order to create tense set-pieces, endanger your hero and allow him to strut his stuff. To further highlight your hero you may want to set up a few expendable goodies, too.

The confrontation with the brain baddie or arch-villain is a scene you should keep for the end, or near the end, of the story, and is a moment to be exploited as much as possible for drama. Whether you want to kill off your chief baddie or keep him alive for future use (you could always cripple him or mutilate him in some way – only writers get to do this to people with impunity) is up to you. Once the brain has been neutralised or brought to justice, any remaining brawn baddies will usually scatter in panic without their leader.

Workshop for Chapter 4

➤ Invent a character, or think about a character you have already devised. Looking back at the example of Luc Simon in this chapter, think about your character's back-story. What would be the most effective ways of presenting the character's background information when you introduce him or her to the reader for the first time?

➤ Using the example of a character you know already, or thinking up a new one, consider what 'journey' they take during the course of the story. Have they changed, and how? What have they learned, and what personal qualities have been brought out? Think of how you would describe the arc of this character from points A to Z of the storyline.

➤ Create a profile for a villain. Why are they bad? What is their motivation? Were they ever a better person, and what might have made them deviate from a more virtuous path?

➤ Think of some good names for characters, both male and female. What kinds of characters do these names suggest to you?

Impact

THE GRABBER

See what you think of this opening.

> Chapter 1
> **Funeral**
>
> Not many people had turned up. Well, surprise surprise.
>
> I sighed and looked around me – first at the panoramic blue sky and then at the ground below me. It was the flat field, out on the fringe of town beyond the primary school and the new housing estate, where they'd been laying the dead away ever since St Andrews' crumbly old churchyards had got so choked with deceased residents' remains that you couldn't so much as put shovel to dirt without rooting up some reluctant skull or jagged bony cage, like the carcass of an old boat, that in all probability had once belonged to the ancestor of someone you knew.

The new graveyard was relatively unoccupied. In one corner I noticed a squat wooden hut, which I took to be the abode of some person employed to look after things, to keep the two acres of lawn neat and prim, to stop people pinching the bunches of flowers laid at the graves and to fork out the daisies that were relentlessly pushed up by the field's sombre tenants. You know, I could have fancied a nice quiet little job like that. Too late now, obviously.

You *might* have guessed that the narrator/main character here is actually dead and has come back as a ghost to watch his own funeral, but it's not immediately clear. What is clear, however, is that this opening scene lacks impact. Look at the 100-word chunk that comprises most of the second paragraph. Reading that, at this very early stage of the story, is like sitting down to dinner and then ramming half your steak into your mouth in one go – tough, chewy and indigestible. As an opener, this hints at some kind of mystery, and the reader *might potentially* want to know more . . . but the desperately overwritten first paragraphs are going to put many people off.

Now look at this one.

Chapter 1

'Daddy, I'm tired,' the little girl in the red pants and the green blouse said fretfully. 'Can't we stop?'

'Not yet, honey.'

He was a big, broad-shouldered man in a worn and scuffed corduroy jacket and plain brown twill slacks. He and the little girl were holding hands and walking up Third Avenue in New York City, walking fast, almost running. He looked over his shoulder and the green car was still there, crawling along slowly in the curbside lane.

'Please, Daddy. Please.'

He looked at her and saw how pale her face was. There were dark circles under her eyes. He picked her up and sat her in the crook of his arm, but he didn't know how long he could go on like that. He was tired, too. And Charlie was no lightweight anymore.

It was 5.30 in the afternoon and Third Avenue was clogged. They were crossing streets in the upper sixties now, and these cross streets were both darker and less populated . . . But that was what he was afraid of.

This opening has everything. It sets the scene clearly without excessive description, and it gives us a very vivid impression of the characters – you know exactly where you are and who you're with. These characters are worn out, stressed out, on the run from something. From what? Who's driving the green car, and what do they want? What's going on? Right from the first line, you're hooked and you want to know more. The sentences are short and tight, and the writing has flow. It's not trashy writing, but it's economical and unflowery. It tells you exactly what you need to know, no more, no less.

Decision time

Right. You're in an airport bookshop, and you've got two minutes before your flight's due to be called. Two minutes to choose the book that'll keep you company across the Atlantic, buy it and hurry off to catch your plane. You're standing there clutching the two books whose openers you've just read, one in each hand. Which one are you going to choose, based on the way they open? Are you going to take a chance on the first one, and hope that it gets easier-going after a few pages, gets more exciting? Maybe it will . . . then again maybe it won't.

Or are you going to go for the one that's already grabbed you and set the scene in such fine style? Obviously, the latter. And that's why Stephen King's *Firestarter*, from which this second sample is taken, was a huge bestseller . . . whereas the first sample you read never got published at all, never even got close.

Get to the good stuff fast . . . and keep it coming

One of the most important assets any book can have – and most especially a thriller – is a catchy, hard-hitting, fascinating opener. It's often called *the grabber* because that's ideally what it does – it grabs the reader by the collar, holds them tight and refuses to let them go until the end.

Here's a grabber from another thriller:

> Nathan Rubin died because he got brave. Not the sustained kind of thing which wins you a medal in a war, but the split-second kind of blurting outrage which gets you killed on the street.

That is the excellent opening from Lee Child's 1998 novel, *Die Trying*. It's good, firstly, because it's confidently *cool* in a mid-Atlantic, swaggering Elmore Leonard-ish kind of way. It's direct, punchy and menacing, telling us exactly what we can expect from the next 500 or so pages.

Another good opener is Dan Brown's first few lines of *The Da Vinci Code*:

> Renowned curator Jacques Saunière staggered through the vaulted archway of the museum's Grand Gallery. He lunged for the nearest painting he could see, a Caravaggio. Grabbing the gilded frame, the seventy-six-year-old man heaved the masterpiece toward himself until it tore from the wall and Saunière collapsed backwards in a heap beneath the canvas.

Actually 'renowned curator' is pretty clunky writing, but you soon get over it and the whole spectacle of this old man behaving so bizarrely, tearing grand masters off the walls of the Louvre, makes you want to know more. Especially when you find out he's about to get murdered by a mysterious assassin, and that there's some kind of strange intrigue going on. Brown has increasingly come under attack for his quality of writing, but this opening 'shot' is a real grabber – just weird enough to be intriguing, full of movement, highly visual and very effective.

PACE

If pacing is the storytelling equivalent of aerodynamics, the ideal thriller plot is as smooth and slick as a Ferrari. Nothing should hinder it or slow it down. Your aim is to raise the reader's heart-rate by a couple of notches on the first page and never let it drop down to normal until the end. Just look at the reviews on the back cover of a typical thriller – and remember that these are put there to make people want to read them: *'Non-stop action'* . . . *'Relentlessly fast-paced'* . . . *'A gripping thrill-ride of a book'* . . . *'The momentum never flags'* . . . *'Exhilarating'* . . . get the idea?

Good pacing
Things that encourage good pacing include:

Short, punchy sentences
This should promote a feeling of breathless urgency.

Plenty of urgent action
This includes agonising cliff-hangers.

Something for the characters to worry about
For example, having a sense of anxiety hovering overhead, e.g. racing to save someone in jeopardy, creates tension.

Starting in the middle of a scene
Don't show more than you have to. For instance, showing a character walking into a building, climbing the stairs, knocking on a door and getting into conversation with someone inside the room will tend to slow things down. Instead, think 'film', go directly to the key part of the scene and cut straight into their dialogue. After the first couple of lines of dialogue you can then include a little bit of economical scene-setting to let the reader know where the characters are, e.g. 'The two men were standing in a drab neon-lit office overlooking the railway tracks'.

Bad pacing
Things that can spoil pace include:

Excessive description
For instance, nobody needs to know what an airport lounge looks like, or which pedal makes a car go faster. If a descriptive detail is somehow important to the story (e.g. you're planting a 'seed' that will figure later – like the green car that's been following you, or the man in the red cap who's sitting across the bar apparently reading a paper, but is really a spy), then it's worth keeping. But a lengthy, detailed description of the moon or a beautiful sunset, however poetically you may have expressed it, has no place in a commercial thriller.

Long swathes of dialogue
We'll be talking more about dialogue later on, but the main thing is to keep it practical. Lengthy detailed discussions are out, and anything too technical will bore the reader. Adhere to the 'need to know' principle.

Too many mundane scenes in-between exciting bits
In real life, people go shopping, wash their underwear, visit the bathroom several times a day, brush their teeth and comb their hair and do all manner of intrinsically boring things that have no business cluttering up the lives of your thriller characters. Nobody wants to read about them – it's the very stuff readers want to escape from! Never let a scene be dull. If you can do without it, cut it out. If for some reason it can't be cut, try to find a way to make it more interesting or surprising.

Too many, or overlong, action scenes
Action scenes should be measured out in well-judged doses. Piling up one after another, or making car chases or shoot-outs too long, can become very tedious. The desired effect is to excite the reader, and you do this by keeping exciting scenes going just long enough to hit a certain peak of tension before moving on.

Too many flashbacks or jump-cuts
These tend to interrupt continuity and can irritate the reader who wants to press on and know what's going to happen next. However, don't rule them out altogether: well handled, leaving your main character on a cliff-hanger and teasing the reader by moving away to a whole different scene can create a lot of suspense. There are times when introducing a new plot thread, or even a new character, at just the right moment can make the reader think *'aha, I wonder what's going to happen here'*, heightening their anticipation as the connections come together in their mind; but it has to be handled with care to make it work.

If every so often you cut away from the main action to show mysterious characters making sinister phone calls, preparing a cell, digging a grave, or brewing up some high explosive for some as-yet-unknown-but-definitely-not-nice purpose, the reader's expectations will be raised a notch. Just make sure that the scenes with main characters are much longer, and that these little cutaways are done economically so they don't detract from the main action.

Laboured explanations from baddies
Usually starting something like '*Well, as I'm going to kill you anyway, I might as well spend eight pages telling you in excruciating detail how and why I committed my dreadful deed . . .*' – do try to keep these kinds of scenes to a minimum! Apart from slowing things down, they often don't even make sense – why would you waste time spilling the beans to someone, only to shoot them afterwards?

Fighting the flab
Think of your story as an Olympic athlete, a swimmer or a runner. Everything in an athlete's physique is geared to performance. They don't have spare tyres of flab jiggling around their midriffs, as that would only slow them down or weigh them down. Your scenes, and in fact your whole novel, should be the same – fast and powerful, slim, trim, 6 per cent body fat, anything superfluous ruthlessly cut away. If it has something to contribute, keep it. If it doesn't do anything for the story, lose it.

The courage to cut
Probably one of the hardest things a writer has to get used to doing is the act of cutting bits out. Cuts can be required for a

number of reasons. Something might just not be working, or, as we talked about earlier, a scene may be overlong or slowing down the pace. Passages you really loved and were truly proud of may become victims of the editing knife. Even whole characters can get the chop. It's not easy to do, but you must get used to it.

Further down the road, a publisher may well require you to do some cutting, sometimes purely in order to trim the length of the manuscript rather than due to any specific problem. If you work with an agent, they may also require changes. So swallow hard and learn what it feels like to delete a thousand sweated-over words into cyber-oblivion.

If it's any consolation, even top writers often have to make changes to their work. In fact, very few novels are ever published exactly as they were first written. Some thrillers undergo radical metamorphosis on the road to publication.

The same applies to thrillers on film, and you can learn a great deal about your craft by studying the 'deleted scenes' sections on movie DVDs. You'll see how often film-makers will axe a scene that isn't working, goes on too long or is superfluous to the plot. Even scenes that have cost millions to make may go under the knife; sometimes it may be the director's favourite scene in the film that gets the chop. It's extremely instructive to study when and why this is done, and as some DVD deleted scenes can be played with a director's or screenwriter's commentary, you can even listen to them explaining their reasons for such cuts. In virtually every case, it's about making the story as slick and as stream-lined as possible.

Chapter length

There are no real rules regarding how long chapters should be, but for a commercial thriller you should think of them as 'bite-size pieces'. Many thrillers have 60 or more chapters, an average of, say, eight pages each for a good-sized novel. Chapters aren't all the same length, though, and you shouldn't try to write to a set number of words or pages. If you envisage a chapter like a scene in a film, you should quickly get a feel for when it needs to come to a close. Applying the film-maker's rule of 'enter each scene late and leave early' helps to keep the pace moving along.

To quote one leading literary agent who specialises in top-notch thrillers:

> [Popular thrillers] work because the action moves so fast, it's rarely long winded with short, episodic chapters that end on a hook or a high point.

Short chapters encourage healthy momentum in a thriller, and they also appeal to readers who may be grabbing moments to read during lunch breaks, on trains and bus queues and waiting rooms. After a hard day's work when they flop into bed at night, they'll be glad of a short chapter they can put away in 20 minutes or less before sleep gets them.

An effective chapter layout used effectively by many writers is to subdivide chapters into shorter numbered chunks. These chunks may be little more than half a page in length, allowing the reader to move quickly from scene to scene just as they would in a film.

TENSE, MODE AND VIEWPOINT

In your planning stages, you need to decide early on how your story is going to be told.

Tense

You could, if desired, choose to write your novel in the present tense, or – as Iain Banks did with his thriller *Complicity* – mix up your tenses to have sections written in the past tense and others written in the present. This can be an interesting narrative technique, and a highly inventive and bold writer like Banks will be able to control and exploit it to its full advantage. However, most thrillers are written in just the past tense. This is what your readers will be most comfortable with, and you would be well advised to do the same.

Experimenting with techniques more normally found in a 'literary' novel may be off-putting to a reader whose normal diet is one of commercial thrillers. My personal advice to you is not to do anything too weird or unconventional such as mixing up past and present tense, having different characters speaking from a first-person 'I' narrative, etc. You could risk putting publishers off an otherwise very good idea.

Modes

There are various modes you can write your novel in, which create different types of atmosphere and give you different tools to work with. Mode is really about viewpoint.

First-person mode

The realisation sent me reeling. McPherson had been lying all along. Struggling to collect my thoughts, I reached for the phone. I heard McPherson's gravel voice on the other end: 'Is that you, Smith?'

The first person can be a good way to tell a story, and it works very well for a more psychological novel, allowing you to open up the protagonist/narrator's thoughts more fully to the reader.

One quite serious limitation to this approach, though – and one that will potentially affect the thriller quite badly – is that once you commit to this mode of narrative the 'camera' will be forced to remain with the protagonist, the 'I' character, throughout the story. That means you can't whisk the reader away to other scenes with other characters showing what intrigues may be going on in the background. You will also be unable to include any flashback passages, and will be limited in your ability to explore the back-story or psychology of other characters such as villains. It *could* be done; it would have to be done through dialogue with your hero, or by your hero discovering information about those other characters. But the first-person mode makes you less fluid, less flexible.

You should also bear in mind that the first-person narrative ties your reader to the same character for the entire story. Is your character appealing enough and interesting enough to spend that whole journey with?

Third-person mode

The realisation sent Smith reeling. McPherson had been lying all along. Struggling to collect his thoughts, he reached for the phone. He heard McPherson's gravel voice on the other end: 'Is that you, Smith?'

Authorial mode

The realisation sent Smith reeling. McPherson had been lying all along. Struggling to collect his thoughts, he reached for the phone.

Far away, McPherson snatched up the receiver. 'Is that you, Smith?', he rumbled in his gravel voice.

If you look at the two examples above, you can see the distinction between the authorial mode and a more restricted third-person mode. The authorial mode allows you to switch the viewpoint, or 'move the camera', away from the main character(s) and show what's going on elsewhere, behind the scenes or in a completely different setting. Just like in a movie, you are free to cut from one short scene to another, even for a few seconds, and then cut back again if needed. This allows enormous freedom and suits the thriller genre very well.

For instance, imagine what might happen next in this scenario, after our characters Smith and McPherson have had their phone discussion:

McPherson quietly replaced the receiver in its cradle and leaned back in his chair, his face twisted in thought. He reached to the desk in front of him, slid open a drawer and stared at the loaded revolver that lay inside.

Now, that short but crucial little scene couldn't be there if we were using a first-person or regular third-person narrative.

Because we would be tied to Smith's viewpoint, virtually handcuffed to the character and unable to go and explore what's going on somewhere else, we'd have no idea that McPherson was obviously contemplating some kind of nasty business as a result of the phone call. We'd have to wait until Smith found out for himself, and the wait could be a dull one.

Thanks to the authorial mode's ability to switch from one setting to another, the reader will now know something that Smith doesn't necessarily know – that *something is going to happen*. And that knowledge, however vague, generates tension. Your reader will want to know whether McPherson is planning to kill Smith. If they have empathy for Smith, that will concern them greatly. Or maybe McPherson is planning to shoot someone else? Maybe he's contemplating suicide? Who knows? (I don't.) But the unanswered question is what creates suspense, and what gives your reader the incentive to turn the page . . . as long as you've done your job and the reader actually *cares* what McPherson might have in store for Smith. If your reader is capable of closing the book at this point, something's wrong.

SURPRISE, SUSPENSE AND THE TWIST

Surprise versus suspense

The authorial mode helps you to generate more suspense because it lets you provide information to the reader that the characters don't know. The master of suspense, Alfred Hitchcock, knew this very well. In his fascinating interviews with fellow film director, Francois Truffaut, he described the difference between surprise and suspense.

The bomb under the table

Imagine, Hitchcock said, two characters are sitting at a table having an innocent conversation. Nothing out of the ordinary is happening. Suddenly, there is the BOOM of an explosion, and the audience realises that there was a bomb under the table. That comes as a surprise, but before the explosion happened the scene was really quite ordinary and unremarkable.

Now, Hitchcock said, imagine the same scenario, the two people having their conversation unaware of the presence of the bomb . . . but with the difference that this time the audience *knows it's there*. How do they know? Because they saw it being planted by a villain earlier – they have been granted access to information that the characters haven't. The audience further knows that the bomb is due to go off at one o'clock precisely, and to crank up their tension even more there is a clock visible on the wall, ticking . . . ticking . . . while the hapless characters are talking. The audience knows that if the characters hang around too long, they're going to get blown up. They're longing to be able to warn the characters of the impending danger, and feeling frustrated that they can't.

In the first case, Hitchcock explains, we have managed to generate a few seconds of *surprise* at the moment of the explosion. In the second case, simply because we allowed the audience to know something the characters didn't, we have cranked this surprise up to generate several *minutes* of *suspense.*

When is a surprise better than suspense? When it's a twist

At a certain point in *The Fulcanelli Manuscript*, I wanted a scene where the villain, the psychopathic religious maniac, Franco Bozza, pops up suddenly to threaten our hero, Ben Hope, when we thought Ben had killed him earlier. Bozza's sudden and unexpected return is a shattering moment for the hero, coming at a point where all seems lost.

This scene was a subject of much indecision. The debate with the scene wasn't whether Bozza should return or not – it was whether or not the reader should know what the hero didn't – that Bozza wasn't dead after all. There was a short scene written that showed the villain had survived his fall off a cliff and was now coming after the hero. With the scene in place, there was the suspense for the reader that the hero was being stalked unawares by this very nasty character. With the scene taken out, the villain's sudden reappearance at the worst possible moment was a much better surprise.

In the end, I elected to go for surprise over suspense. This was for two reasons: firstly, because the hero's activities in the meantime were already providing enough excitement for the reader – there was no real need to generate the extra tension using suspense. Secondly, the surprise, when it came, was also a *twist* that sent the story moving in a new direction.

A good thriller should have more twists and turns than a plate of spaghetti. A twist is where a surprising incident takes the story off in a new and (hopefully) unexpected direction: a dead guy turns out to be anything but; or a goodie turns out to be a baddie; or someone you thought was a baddie turns out to be a goodie (e.g. undercover agent), with the added psychological spice that the main character has mistrusted them and now realises their mistake. That can lead you in all sorts of directions.

The roller-coaster ride

The main role of the twist is to keep the story from ever getting stale. It should be constantly throwing up unexpected new developments, always moving, always keeping your reader guessing at every step. Just as driving down a straight, wide motorway can get boring after a while, taking your reader down too many straight paths, where they can see a long way ahead, will soon result in their finding your story predictable and dull. If at any point it seems the reader might be able to tell what's about to happen make something different happen instead.

Don't be afraid to throw everything into confusion. Let them build up their false hopes, and just when they're not expecting it, pull the rug out from under them – in just the same way as people pay good money to be terrified by a roller-coaster ride, your readers will love you for it!

KEEP THE READER GUESSING

Modern readers are very story-literate and extremely astute when it comes to anticipating the big revelation that you thought you'd kept so well under wraps! The typical thriller reader may not have been raised on high-class lit, but don't ever underestimate them – they are *not* stupid. A lifetime of thrillers and movies and trying to guess the killer's identity in TV 'whodunnit' mysteries has made them very smart and hard to fool. The reader is every bit as streetwise as a hard-boiled detective, and it's your job to stay several steps ahead of them.

Giving it away

A storyline that gives too much away, too quickly, is like a deflated balloon – limp, flaccid and useless, all tension gone. As in a game of poker, the skilful thriller writer will keep his or her cards close to their chest. But not *too* close: guard against keeping them so close that nobody understands what's going on and the readers all give up trying to follow the scanty clues. What does the reader actually *need* to know? You need to maintain a controlled drip-feed of key information that keeps the reader hooked and their curiosity aroused, but just mystified enough not to be able to predict what's coming next. This balancing-act is crucial if the story is to remain engaging and surprising.

Very often in thrillers, a character is not what they first appear to be: even the most apparently earnest and helpful ally or long-time friend can turn out to be a treacherous murderer. You, the creator of the story and characters, have known this from the start – but the question is, at what point should you let the reader in on the secret? Consider the following two examples:

Example 1:
'Hey, Bill – I really owe you one there,' John said. 'You've saved my life, buddy.'

Bill chuckled into the phone. 'Come on, what are friends for?' he said. 'You'd have done the same for me. Now take my advice and get out of there.'

After he put the phone down, Bill thought for a moment, then picked it up again and dialled a different number. 'He's still there', he said. 'You'd better move fast.'

Example 2:
'Hey, Bill – I really owe you one there,' John said. 'You've saved my life, buddy.'

Bill chuckled into the phone. 'Come on, what are friends for?' he said. 'You'd have done the same for me. Now take my advice and get out of there.'

After he put the phone down, Bill thought for a moment, then picked it up again and dialled a different number.

In the first example, we see that John's trust in Bill is perhaps less grounded than John thinks – Bill is obviously up to something, and seems to be giving John away to someone who may have bad intentions. The reader is allowed to see this, and will be able to predict that this betrayal will have a negative outcome for John. The reader will now know not to trust Bill, and knows something that John doesn't know. This is fine, if that's what the writer intends; however, depending on where this scenario takes place, and how important Bill is as a character, the writer gives away this information at the risk of losing the tension in the plot.

The second example gives far less away. Here, Bill's role in the situation seems more ambiguous. When he picks up the phone a second time, it could just be to phone his wife to remind her to let the cat out . . . or it *could* be to tell the baddies where John is. We don't know. The mystique has been preserved and the reader's mind is working hard, trying to figure out whether we can trust Bill or not. Maybe it's a red herring, playing on our cynical expectations that an old friend probably *will* turn out rotten . . . who can say? The only way to find out is to keep reading.

Keeping the reader on their toes and guessing a little is an essential part of good thriller storytelling. Sometimes, all this takes is a little trimming away of excess information as in the second example above.

SEX AND VIOLENCE

No discussion of impact in a thriller is complete without considering those good old staples of the genre, sex and violence. Many first-time writers agonise endlessly over their handling of these sometimes delicate scenes.

To show or not to show?

How graphic you want to be with either is really up to you. The sliding scale between eroticism and pornography also has its counterpart in violence. At one end of the scale you can merely suggest:

As I walked away from the building, I heard the single flat report of the gun from inside and I knew Forrester was dead.

Or you can go to the other extreme and show everything:

I watched through the window as Forrester put the gun to his temple, screwed his eyes shut and pulled the trigger. His skull burst open like a ripe melon, and blood and brains exploded over the wall.

For many readers, the first version would possibly be more effective. More is sometimes less, and it may not be necessary to go for the technicolour gross-out. It's surprising how much the imagination will fill in. Much has been made of the infamous ear-cutting scene in Quentin Tarantino's film *Reservoir Dogs*, where a bound victim has his ear razored off by a grinning psycho villain. Many people will tell you how sickened they were by this gruesome sight, and yet if you watch the film you'll see that at the key moment the camera actually averts its eye and you only hear the scream. Sometimes you can create a more powerful effect when the worst of the violence takes place offstage.

Sex is just the same – a strap off the shoulder can be sexier than actual exposed body parts. Not every reader will want to read graphic sex scenes. Whatever you opt for, do try to avoid using any of the more cringe-making euphemisms that some writers resort to: coy expressions like '*his engorged manhood*', '*he touched her secret parts*' and '*she could see he was ready for her*' are just plain awful. I would rather see Forrester blow his brains out!

We're all grown-ups, and thrillers cater for an adult market. If you want to show sex, show it; if not, cast a few shadows on the wall and let the reader imagine it.

But make it quick

However graphically you decide to depict sex and/or violence, don't keep the scenes running for too long. This isn't for censorious reasons but purely in the interests of pacing – sex scenes, fights, gun battles, car chases and the like can all become monotonous if allowed to drone on.

THE END

The ending of a story is almost as important as the beginning. A thriller novel should generally end on an upbeat note. Having played with their emotions for a few hours, cranked up the tension and hopefully kept them up late at night unable to put the book down, we leave the reader with a feeling of satisfaction, the way they might feel after a fine dinner or a great movie.

Keep it clear

Unresolved or ambiguous endings have no place in a commercial thriller. Baddies should be brought down (at least temporarily) and goodies should prevail (though perhaps rather torn and battered). Heroes get girls and vice-versa, just causes win over unjust ones, good triumphs over evil. The thriller follows the same conventions as its cousin the horror story, nearly always resolving itself quite conservatively by restoring the status quo in some way. The threat is averted, the vampire has been staked, the world's a better place and we can all sleep soundly in our beds.

Tie it up neatly

In a complicated storyline there may be quite a number of loose ends that need to be tied up by the end. You should be starting to tie these up some time *before* the end; otherwise what can happen is the 'bottleneck' situation where everything has to be explained in a rush in the final few scenes, creating a hectic and often overwhelmingly detailed ending with too many long explanations. Writers struggling with these intricate conclusions can often forget to tie up some of the loose ends, and the whole thing gets messy and unwieldy. Readers will be more satisfied by a straightforward ending that glides smoothly to a climax, delivers a final burst of excitement and then comes to a close: the hero rides into the sunset and we can finally lay the book down with a big contented sigh.

Workshop for Chapter 5

➤ Write a 'grabber' opening for a story. Alternatively, if you have already started writing your own thriller, look back at the opening and consider whether it could be made more punchy and exciting.

➤ In any book you have read recently, did you notice the pace slackening off excessively at any point? Was it ever boring? Try to analyse where and why the pace might have flagged, and think of ways you would solve the problem if it were your book.

➢ Experiment with modes: take a short scene (no more than a paragraph or two) from a novel or something you might have written yourself, and try writing different first-person, third-person and authorial versions. Which seems most effective and would suit the story best?

➢ Think back to a thriller you read recently. If it contained any love scenes or scenes of violence, were these shown in graphic detail or more hinted at? Would you have handled these scenes differently?

⑥

Language, Style and Dialogue

MASTERING THE ART OF LANGUAGE

While a film-maker has many tools at their disposal and can affect their audience using visual images, sound and music, those of us in the literary world only have one. We depend entirely on *language* to stimulate the reader's imagination and engage them in our story. If we only have one tool, we need to know how to use it properly.

Grammar and punctuation

For many people, these two terms are guaranteed to bring up unpleasant schooldays memories. Unimaginative and uninspiring schoolteachers are largely responsible for giving grammar and punctuation such an undeservedly fearsome reputation. In fact they're nothing to be afraid of, just a set of simple conventions that enable us to hang words together in a recognisable way in order to put information across. When writers ignore these conventions, whether it's because they can't be bothered to abide by them, or they believe it's 'cool' or 'literary' to flout the rules, or they just didn't *know* the rules, the result is predictable. Bad grammar and punctuation lead not only to bad sentences but to beautifully written rejections from agents and publishers.

If you need to brush up on the nuts and bolts of language, there are plenty of grammar books available to help you. As well as studying these, the best place to study the applied use of language is by reading books. Instead of just letting the meaning of the words wash over you, study how they've been put together. Why did the writer put in a semi-colon here instead of a comma? Why did they structure that sentence that way? You'll soon see that it's really very simple, and that there's nothing to fear from the mechanics of language.

Breaking the rules

Once you know the rules, you can safely break a few of them. Thrillers seldom contain any kind of writing that's 'literary' or experimental, but you'll see that certain rules are thrown out from time to time. Most often flouted is the old rule our teachers hammered into us that one should always write in complete sentences, that is, that each sentence should contain a subject, verb and object (*Johnny kicked the ball. The car hit the tree.*) or, at least, a subject and a verb (*Johnny ran. The car skidded.*).

Here's a nice example of a writer who knows the rules but breaks them to good effect:

> In the flesh he was mostly unremarkable. Not big, not small. Maybe six feet, maybe two hundred pounds. Grey hair, not thin, not thick, not short, not long. He was about fifty.
>
> (*Persuader,* Lee Child)

Five sentences. Only two complete ones. Technically ungrammatical. But very effective. Get the idea?

Adjectives and adverbs

Be sparing with these. There is no point in piling up four adjectives if you can use one good noun instead. Likewise, think twice before you spoil a perfectly good sentence by gluing adverbs to a verb – just make the verb stronger.

Johnny threw the stone <u>angrily</u> (adverb) at Bobby.

Better to say instead:

Johnny hurled the stone at Bobby.

Don't agonise too much over these points as you write up your first draft, as you have more important issues to deal with at that stage. Later on, comb through what you've written and see how many unnecessary adjectives and adverbs you can prune from your writing. You'll see what a difference it makes.

One of the most important places to cut out adverbs is in the dialogue attribution, the '*he said/she replied*' bits that show who said what. Here's an example:

'I hate you! I wish you were dead!' Jenny shouted furiously.

Jenny's sentiments are so clear from her dialogue that the adverb 'furiously' hangs like a millstone around the neck of the sentence. Cut out the adverb, upgrade the verb from 'shouted' to 'screamed', and you have something much cleaner and more effective.

Let's see if we can apply the same rule to something a little more meaty.

> 'You're going down, Jones,' Smith growled angrily, pointing the .45.
> 'Please don't kill me,' Jones pleaded imploringly.
> 'Put the pistol down, Smith,' Brown snapped urgently from across the warehouse as the gunman took aim.

This kind of over-writing belongs in one of those trashy pulp novels I can remember buying as a child for 18 pence in Woolworths. Look how much stronger it gets below, just by taking out those horrid adverbs:

> 'You're going down, Jones,' Smith growled, pointing the .45.
> 'Please don't kill me,' Jones pleaded.
> 'Put the pistol down, Smith,' Brown snapped from across the warehouse as the gunman took aim.

Still not great, but getting there. Now let's sweep through it again and clean up the dialogue attribution verbs, the 'growled', 'pleaded' and 'snapped'. They're not only corny, they're completely redundant as the dialogue itself tells you everything. Try this:

> 'You're going down, Jones.' Smith pointed the .45.
> 'Please don't kill me,' Jones said.

'Put the pistol down, Smith,' Brown yelled from across the warehouse as the gunman took aim.

Better now? Not perfect, but much better. This keeps the dialogue attribution verbs toned down. There's no need to have Jones *plead* as his line says it all, and we can imagine clearly enough how he feels with the gun to his head. As for Brown, he needs to do more than just *speak* his line, in order to convey his sense of urgency, so we can replace 'snapped' with the less florid 'yelled'. We now have a piece of writing that looks much cleaner to the eye and flows far more nicely than the monstrosity we started out with a page ago.

Style

Different writers can have radically different styles depending on their use of vocabulary and sentence structure. Consider this passage:

> Noon dinner, Foley took his pork butts and yams down the center aisle looking for Chino among all the white T-shirts and dark hair. There he was, at a table of his little-guy countrymen eating macaroni and cheese, a dish Foley had passed on in the chow line. Jesus, eating a pile of it.
>
> (*Out of Sight*, Elmore Leonard)

Now this one:

> The thought that he might never see her again could be dismissed as a delusion, an absurd over-reaction, to an excess of solitude and silence. And from the notion that, at any second, she would return, calling to him as she

came down the track, part of his mind could not be dislodged: the orderly, housetrained, rational part.

(*Into the Blue*, Robert Goddard)

It would be a very amusing exercise to rewrite these passages, each in the style of the other. To my own tastes, Leonard's is a light soufflé, while Goddard's is a stodgy pudding. There's no objective measure of which is *better*, although I think it would be harder to emulate Leonard's writing than Goddard's.

Style is partly what a writer is born with, and partly what they develop through years of writing. Your background, the people you grow up with, the books you read as a child, your education (to a certain degree) and the things you want to write about will all variously influence your style. This doesn't mean that you have to have been part of the criminal underworld, or a tough jailbird, to write about them convincingly – Elmore Leonard is an English literature graduate, not a Folsom ex-con.

Your style will develop as you gain experience as a writer. Until your distinctive voice emerges you shouldn't try to copy other writers' styles. Many writers have tried, and failed, to emulate the great Elmore Leonard, for instance. If you are true to yourself and write with passion and sincerity, your personal voice will inevitably shine through sooner or later.

THE CLICHÉ

A cliché is, simply, any expression that is too obvious, that we've all seen too many times before. Hackneyed expressions like 'he was walking on air', 'a hail of bullets', 'you could have knocked me over with a feather', 'she was cut to the quick', 'the table groaned under the weight', 'he was purple with rage' and a million others, are to be avoided. Agents and publishers will be quick to spot clichés in your writing, and they won't be impressed. Root clichés out mercilessly whenever you find them.

THE ART OF GOOD DIALOGUE

Writing good dialogue is something of a balancing act. It needs to sound unforced and naturalistic, so that the reader can forget that they're reading a book at all, and that they're not hearing a real conversation. On the other hand, it shouldn't be *too* naturalistic. Real life speech is peppered with 'you knows' and 'kind ofs', people repeat themselves or go off at a tangent, and sometimes seldom finish a sentence. So, paradoxically, if you write dialogue that's too real it might be pretty hard to understand.

The best way to learn the art of great dialogue is to study how the very best writers do it. Here's another piece from Leonard's *Out of Sight*:

He was asking Ray, 'Did you pay the guy the reward?'
'Yeah, as soon as we got back.'
'What do you do, write a check?'
'No, we paid it in cash. It was late, the banks were

closed – I asked Santiago if he wanted to keep the money in our safe till tomorrow. You kidding? No way. Skinny old guy with dark skin, he looked like a chicken. He walked out with the ten grand in a shopping bag.'

The beauty of this dialogue is in its rugged simplicity, its sparkling lightness of touch and Leonard's uncanny way of sounding upbeat and laid back at the same time. Whatever type of thriller you write, I urge you to read as much of Elmore Leonard's work as you can.

Keep it uncluttered

Trying to convey too much information through dialogue can give it a very clumsy and stodgy feel. Long, un-broken paragraphs full of technical information, whether it be medical, legal, police or military jargon, can make the reader's eyes begin to glaze over and skip the lines.

By the same token, avoid setting up the story by *telling* it through dialogue. Keep dialogue to a minimum whilst *show-ing* it to the reader. For example, say Jane has had a really bad day – corpses showing up in the bath, earthquakes on the way to work, her boss trying to murder her. That evening she tells her husband all the things that happened to her. But relating all those events through dialogue will seem spooned on and lack impact. It's better to show those events through the action. If you want Jane to tell her husband all about it later, you can skip the details and say something like: 'She told him what had happened in one breathless stream. His frown deepened as he listened'.

Keep it simple

Avoid falling into the trap, as many writers do, of believing that displays of technical virtuosity are the same thing as 'good' writing. They're not, and especially not when it comes to writing dialogue. Fancy or 'educated'-sounding language may work in a formal letter but it positively ruins dialogue. Some examples:

◆ **Don't** write: *'I can spare you half an hour before my presence is called for at the table'*.
◆ **Do** write: *'We'd better make this quick – dinner's at half past'*.

◆ **Don't** write: *'I cannot disclose what she revealed to me; I am sworn to secrecy'*.
◆ **Do** write: *'Sorry, what she told me was private. I'm keeping my mouth shut'*.

◆ **Don't** write: *'He did not apprise me of the full extent of your activities until yesterday'*.
◆ **Do** write: *'He only told me yesterday what you were up to'*.

Keep out the obvious

See how the following passage strikes you.

The paramedics wheeled the stretcher out of the building. A white sheet covered the body head to toe. Where it lay across the upper torso it was slicked with blood. A pallid hand slipped out from under the sheet, and spots of blood left a trail across the pavestones.

'Oh my God!' Janet screamed as she broke free of the

policeman's grip and rushed over to the stretcher, her face lit up in blue from the flashing lights of the ambulance. 'He's dead!'

Yes, Janet, we *know* he's dead. The reader doesn't need to be told, and in real life Janet would be unlikely to volunteer this information. Better just to have her scream, run to the stretcher, have to be restrained by police, and so on.

Fit the dialogue to the character . . .

For the sake of realism some types of characters may need to speak in a particular way. It might be more appropriate for some characters to speak in a more formal style – foreigners, for instance, whose knowledge of English may have come mainly from the classroom (unlike native speakers, who generally learn very little of their language there). Other characters might talk ungrammatically, or have some quirk of speech, or tend to swear a lot. You wouldn't give a tough gangster the same kind of lines to speak as a mild-mannered academic, a shy student or a batty scientist.

. . . But don't stereotype them

Different characters in your story should speak with different voices, just as real living people speak. Avoid matching particular types of characters to particular styles of dialogue, or lapsing into stereotype. Yes, people from different social and professional backgrounds do often tend to speak differently, and yes, you can often tell a lot about a person's education or employment from the way they express themselves. By all means illustrate those differences – but this isn't the same thing as making a university professor spout overblown hyperbole and speak in half-page sentences *just because* he's a university professor, or making a cab driver talk like some wide-boy out of a Guy Ritchie movie *just because* he's a cab driver.

Of course, if there's a valid reason for them to speak that way – for instance if you're making a point of showing that the university professor is a pompous jackass who enjoys using long words nobody can understand – then go for it but make it interesting, and don't get carried away.

BAD LANGUAGE, SLANG AND FOREIGN EXPRESSIONS

Swearing

Swearing is an art form, and for many writers has become a living and integral part of our language – although regrettably I am unable to give you any nice examples here! There are those who can do it with great flair and wit, such as the screenwriter/film director, Quentin Tarantino, and the Scottish comedian Billy Connolly. On other lips it can sound trashy and vulgar, or stilted and affected.

So-called 'bad' language can add a lot of colour and flavour to writing of a certain style, but it's not for everyone and doesn't suit every environment. Some writers feel rather self-conscious about including 'naughty' words in their writing (one lady told me she felt as though her mother, who was long since dead, was looking over her shoulder all the time as she wrote). Writers have to be relaxed with the style they use. If the use of swearing is going to make your characters' dialogue sound stilted and artificial, if you don't feel natural with it, then just don't use it. There is no rule dictating a thriller shall contain swear-words, and many writers (such as Robert Goddard) seldom or never use them. No book has ever shot to the top of the bestseller list simply because it was full of foul or obscene language; and no amount of f-words will compensate for sloppy plotting or a lack of tension.

Slang expressions, confusing and dated terms

It can be tempting to want to lend a novel a contemporary flavour by including a lot of slang expressions and 'street talk'. Just remember that expressions that sound hip and trendy now will age rapidly and in a few years' time will have dated as badly as '*dig it*', '*far out*', '*groovy, man!*' and '*he was some cool cat*'.

Other seriously dated expressions include those that will make your dialogue seem like something out of an Enid Blyton novel. '*Gosh, you are a brick*' may have worked in the 1940s but sound as dated now as 'gadzooks' and 'me-thinks'.

Cockney rhyming slang can be an amusing and effective way of portraying a certain type of Londoner. Avoid letting them lapse into out-and-out farce, and steer clear of excesses such as '*blimey, mate, he's only gone and half-inched me bugs bunny*' that may mystify American readers (and a few British ones too). They're also completely untranslatable, so bang goes your overseas market! Similarly, if setting your story in a particular region, avoid overuse of regional dialect or colloquialisms.

Foreign words and phrases

Many thrillers move through a variety of exotic locations. John Case's *The Eighth Day*, for instance, sets its action in the USA, Italy, Turkey and Switzerland. To make the settings seem real and convincing, some writers insert the odd phrase in the language of whatever country the characters are in. This can add a lot of colour to the writing, but be careful not to insert too many foreign expressions as these may confuse or bore the reader and are very likely to put off a publisher.

Four ways to get around this problem are:

1. Translate them (but only very brief snatches). For instance:
   'He was a fascist. *Enas fasistis.*' (*Into the Blue*, Robert Goddard)

2. Bounce the foreign words off another character who doesn't speak the language:
   '*Ich möchte ihn verschiessen,*' muttered Heinrich, staring at Joe.
   'What did he say?' Joe asked Fritz.
   Fritz grinned. 'He said he'd like to shoot you.'

3. Use foreign words whose meanings are easy to guess:
   '*Bastardo! Cretino!*' screamed Luigi. (No translation necessary!)

4. Make it clear from the context:

   '*Tu as l'argent?*' the bald man asked, glancing at the briefcase.

   John set it on the table and flipped the catches. 'Yeah, the money's all in here,' he said.

These simple devices have allowed bits of Greek, German, Italian and French to be inserted without sacrificing clarity, giving the writing that extra little bit of a cosmopolitan feel. If you think it would be effective to make use of foreign phrases but don't feel confident with the language, you may be able to find a native speaker or a languages teacher to help you out.

Workshop for Chapter 6

➤ Look out for passages in books that you feel are overwritten or clumsy. Take note of what you think is wrong with them, and rewrite them accordingly. Then see how your version compares with the original.

➤ Imagine three characters in a situation where they are waiting for something to happen. The three people all have quite different temperaments – one is laid-back and relaxed, one is nervy and impatient, and the third is sullen and moody. Try writing a dialogue-heavy scene around this scenario, imagining how each character's attitude and individual personality is reflected in their dialogue.

➢ Start making an active and conscious habit of rooting out clichés and other literary 'sins' from your own writing. Focus honestly and objectively on aspects of your style that could be improved upon. Don't think of this exercise as self-critique; think of it as product development.

7

Going The Distance

All the elements are in place. You've built your skeleton and begun fleshing out the bare bones. Your characters are developing from their first foetal origins into friends and enemies so real to you that you can almost feel them. The feel and style of the novel are in your head. All you need to do now is write the thing!

THE LONG HAUL

Writing a novel is a long process. Some writers take years to pen their thrillers – for instance Dustin Thomason and Ian Caldwell took six years to write their bestseller *The Rule of Four*. Part of the reason a book may take so long to write is that authors have other commitments to take care of. Caldwell and Thomason were both students for part of the time they were working on their book. Other authors have jobs, children and other distractions to drag them from their writing desk.

The first couple of novels in a writer's career are usually the toughest task. Stephen King wrote his first book *Carrie* while working full-time in an industrial laundry, where his job was wringing maggots out of restaurant tablecloths. If things go well (as they obviously did in Mr King's case), an author can give up the day job to write full-time, and they have much more time to dedicate to their books – as a result they become faster and more prolific.

INITIAL DRAFTS

The first draft . . .

Contrary to what many outsiders seem to think, nobody ever sits down and writes a polished novel straight off from beginning to end. Naturally, every writer will have their preferred way of working, but the usual procedure is to set down a first draft fairly quickly, and then come back and start hammering it into shape.

Don't worry if a first draft seems a bit rough! It's only a prototype, not the finished product. The novel may go through several more drafts before it's ready. Bear this in mind as you go, and avoid the temptation of tinkering with it too much in the initial draft. Forge ahead with it and get to the end. It's like painting a wall – the first coat can be 'slapped on' without too much attention to detail. There might be a few bits of the old colour showing through here and there, but you know they'll be covered up by the next coat.

. . . Then the second

When the first draft is down, you'll be feeling mentally tired. Take a break from the story for a few days – some top authors wait for up to six weeks to freshen their mind before returning to take up their pen again. You might not want, or be able, to wait that long, but it's important to take some kind of a break and let your tired brain recharge its batteries. It also helps you to detach your mind from the story, so that when you return for the next draft you will be more objective and able to see its faults.

With the second draft – like the second coat of paint – you will spend more time paying attention to detail. In the process of writing it, you may realise that certain plot points didn't work or needed changing. The story may change quite considerably as it develops, and some finished novels bear little resemblance to the original plan.

Trimming it down

The second draft should emerge as a trimmer, lighter, shorter version of the first draft. Be tough and cut away anything that isn't absolutely needed. Aim to cut the length down by about 10 per cent – so if the first draft runs to 110,000 words, the second should be around the 100,000 mark. Judicious cutting can work wonders on a manuscript, and you may be quite amazed by how much faster-reading and effective your story becomes.

When you're happy with the second draft, read the whole manuscript through carefully. Printing it off and reading from the paper will allow you to take a break from the computer, as well as to make pencil notes in the margin. Use a fairly large font size, say Times New Roman 14, and print it off 1.5 or double-spaced for easy reading.

Now's the time to get down to some real work. Be honest with yourself, and try to imagine it's someone else's work you're scrutinising. Put yourself into the mindset of a publisher or agent.

◆ What impression does the opening make? Is it a grabber?

◆ Is the reader carried straight into the heart of the story, or do things take ages to get going?

◆ Does every scene have a purpose? Is it doing something for the story?

◆ If not, could you do without it?

◆ Are the events of the plot coming in the best order?

◆ Are the important scenes slotting in at the best points for maximum effect?

◆ Does everything in the storyline make sense? Could anything be unclear or confusing to the reader?

◆ Check for continuity – that the blue jacket stayed blue, and the dead guy stayed dead!

◆ Check for loose ends and things that don't add up.

◆ Are flashbacks or other plot devices interfering with clarity?

◆ Are you giving anything away too soon?

◆ Are you keeping anything back too much?

◆ What is the pacing of the novel like? Are there any points where the pace flags, and things get boring?

◆ Have you done everything you can to keep it 'on the boil?'

- Are there enough twists and surprises to keep the reader engaged?

- How are the characters coming over? Are they real and convincing?

- Do their psychology and motivation tally with their behaviour?

- Would the reader find the hero/heroine appealing?

- Does each main character have a 'journey'?

- Does each character have a sufficiently distinct voice?

- Does each character's dialogue fit them well?

- Is your style consistent throughout the novel?

- Have you avoided the excessive use of adverbs and adjectives?

- Are there any foreign language expressions that are unclear?

- Is dialogue attribution as clean as possible?

- Have you steered clear of dated expressions?

- Is description standing in the way of pace?

- Does the story end in a satisfying way?

- Are all the loose ends tied up properly?

FINAL DRAFT AND POLISH

The last draft of your novel could be the third, or it could be the sixth. This depends entirely on the individual book and how much work it needs to get it up to scratch. Keep honing, keep cutting, keep questioning.

The closer your novel gets to being finished, the more attention you should pay to the little things:

Repetition
Check that words aren't being repeated too often – writers often have their pet expressions that they may re-use without even being aware of it. The computer is a great tool for finding these, by typing the pet phrase into the 'find' box and scanning through the manuscript for it.

Clichés
While you're at it, have a massive 'cliché clearout'. It's worth spending some time sifting backwards and forwards through the manuscript, not trying to read it in any kind of order but keeping an eye open for any clichéd expressions that need rewriting.

Dialogue
Run through all your dialogue to make sure it's zippy and natural. Speak it out loud if that helps, or get other people to act out the scenes with you!

Stray adverbs
Type the words 'he said' into your computer's search facility and trawl through the entire manuscript from start to finish.

This will throw up any stray adverbs you might want to prune from the dialogue attribution ('he said' will also take you to all the 'she saids'). To improve the dialogue attribution still further, run searches to track down and delete all those *he snapped, he drawled, he cried, he grated, he growled, he shrieked*, or (worst of all) *he ejaculated*, that may have slipped in when you weren't paying attention. Get rid of them quickly before someone else reads them!

Check all spelling, grammar and punctuation
Don't trust your computer's spell-checker to make the correct changes. When I ran a spell-check on this book the computer wanted to change the name of publisher Piatkus Books to 'Piteous Books' (which wouldn't look good on a submission letter!).

The tinkering temptation

Hopefully, by the time you're nearly done, the only changes needed will be tiny little things. Make them by all means, but be wary of getting into a tinkering habit. Tinkering, or fiddling about with minor details and wording, is only useful as far as you're actually making worthwhile changes to the novel. Remember that there are a virtually infinite number of ways to word a sentence, and that just because an alternative way of expressing something occurs to you, this doesn't necessarily mean you should change what was written before. Avoid spoiling the fresh, spontaneous feel of your writing by agonising over it too much, and don't be tempted to start inserting adjectives and adverbs all over the place just because you can!

Showing it to other people

At a certain stage you may want to let other people see your work-in-progress. Most usually, these will be family members and close friends. They will probably be at least as excited as you are that you're writing a book, and will be very keen to read it and offer their ideas.

Letting friends and family read your work can be a good thing, or not such a good thing. It's a good thing if:

◆ They are experienced thriller readers and understand what the genre requires.

◆ They can give you an objective appraisal of your book.

◆ They aren't afraid of telling you its faults.

It's less of a good thing if:

◆ They don't normally read thrillers and are only reading this one because you wrote it.

◆ They don't really know what you're expecting of them as critics.

◆ They're inclined to tell you what they think you want to hear, i.e. that this is the most riveting thing since *The Da Vinci Code* and you're bound to sell millions of copies of it.

Unfortunately, the latter is more usually the case. Your friends and family have the best of intentions, and it's only natural that they should want to support and encourage you. However, be realistic about the value of their comments.

Just because Uncle Fred loved your story, this doesn't mean that a hardened literary agent will be so easily impressed.

WRITER'S BLOCK

Writer's block is when the creative flow seems to stutter and then comes to a grinding halt. If you find you're dried up, you might try some of these ideas:

◆ Stop writing for a while. Staring at the screen won't help, and nor will trying to force the words out of yourself.

◆ Don't be over-critical of your work. Nobody gets it right first time, or even second time! Even established authors might have to do five re-writes of their novel before it's publishable.

◆ Take a fresh look at something totally different. Try sketching out a new plot for something else.

◆ Read a book instead, not actively looking for ideas. Something may come to you.

◆ Do some other activities, like sports, cycling, golf, whatever you enjoy. A creative mind is a relaxed mind.

Does writer's block really exist?

Many writers don't believe that such a thing as writer's block really exists. It may be that this 'syndrome' is only a reflection of the fact that writing can sometimes be arduous and challenging! If that's the case, 'writer's block' is no different from any of the challenges facing anyone in day-to-day life. The fact is that anything worth achieving is always going to present difficulties. We either get over them, or we let them overcome us.

'The yips'

More serious writer's block may be a psychological difficulty, such as the absolute conviction that you're *incapable* of doing something. Golfers call this chronic lack of confidence 'the yips'.

The composer Rachmaninov suffered so badly from the musical equivalent of writer's block and 'the yips' that at a certain point he had to go to a hypnotist to be cured of the deep conviction that he simply couldn't compose any longer. And it worked!

Writers who suffer from a general lack of self-esteem will find that perseverance breeds a sense of achievement, which in turn builds into a feeling of confidence. Make the effort to write just a few lines each day.

◆ Don't force yourself to write all day long.

◆ Don't sit there staring helplessly at a blank page or screen.

◆ Don't agonise over what you've written, or try to scrutinise it too hard.

◆ Don't go around telling everyone you've got writer's block. The more you repeat it, the more you'll believe it, and the more it will be true.

◆ DO think positively. *Writer's block? Me?*

THE POWER OF POSITIVE THINKING

Don't let negative thoughts drag you down! Stay positive and focused, and believe in yourself. You've come this far, and with the right professional attitude you'll see it through. You've made a commitment, and you're vowed to honour it. Other people have, and so can you.

Hold on to the thought that what you're doing is special and worthwhile. Any time you feel down, stuck or demoralised during the long haul of writing your novel, remind yourself that every famous author was once in exactly the same position as you, and sometimes a lot worse. Think of poor old Stephen King and his maggots. He believed in himself, persevered, and before too long those maggots were history.

Thoughts to write by

◆ *Love the challenge of the moment, whatever it may be.*

◆ *Before you start writing, visualise what you want to see on the page.*

◆ *You control your destiny.*

◆ *Success is a combination of process and perseverance.*

◆ *A confident writer thinks about what he wants to happen. A writer who lacks confidence thinks about what he doesn't want to happen.*

◆ *Good preparation breeds confidence. You are prepared.*

◆ *Dwelling on a problem only compounds it.*

◆ *When you maintain a positive attitude, setbacks won't bother you.*

◆ *Giving up is not an option.*

When it's just not working

Sometimes writers get blocked for reasons directly relating to the story – for instance, when you can't see your way out of a plot situation, or you can't see how to make a scene work. This may be a problem you didn't foresee when planning the storyline – most novels will deviate and wander from the plan as writing progresses. Now, part of the thriller-writing process is placing heroes in difficult situations and then having to find inventive, surprising but believable ways of getting them out again. But what if you can't? You've pinned your main character in a fiendish spot from which there seems to be no escape. The reader will be expecting you to come up with the goods, but no amount of head-scratching will produce an escape route in your overheated imagination. Help! It would be so easy to get badly blocked at this point. Here are some tips to help you get out of it:

Watch a thriller movie with similar themes
I'm not suggesting that you should be tempted to copy! But often a scene in a film may inspire you to come up with something. You should be able to disguise it enough to avoid any cries of 'rip-off!'. I've done this several times, but I'm not going to tell you where! One example I *haven't* used is the great device in Hitchcock's *North by Northwest* where Cary Grant manages to escape from the baddies at a public auction. There's no way out – the baddies are guarding the

door. So Grant starts heckling the auctioneer and making such a nuisance of himself that the police are called and he is arrested. This was exactly what he wanted, and the only way to escape from the villains. This kind of device can easily be adapted to a different scenario to offer your hero a way out.

Ask advice from a friend you can trust
Sometimes an objective outsider, coming at it with a fresh mind and not bogged down in the complexities of your story, can come up with a brilliant idea. People with particular jobs or skills may be able to provide useful technical or practical solutions to the problem.

Just leave it and go away and write another part of the story you feel more comfortable with
Remember you can write the story in any order you like if you're working to some kind of plot plan. It will help to freshen up your mind, and maybe something will jump out at you from nowhere.

See if it's possible to go back and plant a seed
Write something into the story that will help you resolve the problem. For instance, in James Cameron's script of the movie *The Abyss* (one of the most gripping thrillers ever made), the main character is having problems with his marriage and in a fit of anger he symbolically hurls his wedding ring down a chemical toilet. Then, suddenly regretting his action, he fishes it out again, getting stained blue to the elbow, and puts it on. Later on, that ring saves his life. Watch the movie and see how there was *no* way he could have survived if he hadn't put that ring back on.

Set the scene with music

As a writer I find that having different types of music on in the background can help create different types of ambiance and allow ideas to start trickling into my mind. This holds for all stages of the writing process. Late one night I was writing quite a gothic scene, where an old priest is confronted by a lunatic at night in a medieval churchyard. It wasn't easy getting into the feel of the scene, when suddenly over the radio came an amazing piece of music – *Litany* by the contemporary composer Arvo Pärt – that with its spookily-edged, beautiful but unsettling feel, took me straight into the heart of the scene and made it work. There would have been no way to write that scene listening to jazz! Perhaps because we're so used to the way music creates part of the atmosphere in a movie, simply listening to the right music can take us halfway there. Later in the same novel, Eric Satie provided the piano soundtrack for lonely, contemplative scenes with the main character; while Jimi Hendrix and Miles Davis's abrasive fusion jazz powered some of the action scenes, shootouts and car chases!

LETTING GO

At a certain point, when you've checked everything you can possibly think of, and when no matter how ruthlessly objective you are your novel seems to be ready, you're going to have to take a deep breath and let go of it. Stop tinkering, and prepare to release it into the big, bad world where it belongs! This step can take a surprising amount of courage, but remind yourself that this moment is what your novel was born for. Believe in it.

Workshop for Chapter 7

➤ For an outside perspective on how writers face the challenges of their profession, read some biographies or (probably better) autobiographies of well-known authors, e.g. Stephen King's semi-autobiographical book On Writing where he relates his early experiences of trying to break through in the publishing world. You could also look through magazines such as Writing, where published authors often talk frankly about their own difficulties and the obstacles they have overcome to write their novels.

➤ If you're a member of a writing group, discuss with other group members how they have overcome problems such as writer's block or other barriers to finishing a long piece of writing. This topic would make a very good group discussion.

8

Getting It Out There

You've finally finished your manuscript? Good, now it's time to start thinking about how best to present it to the outside world. It's tough out there, so it's vitally important to package and present your work as best you can.

PSEUDONYMS

As a thriller writer, you have the chance to reinvent yourself to some degree. What is your image going to be? How is this going to be reflected in your chosen pen-name? A writer of tough, hard-hitting thrillers with a brooding photo on the back cover wouldn't have a name like, say, Archibald Peabottom.

One very good reason for using a pseudonym is if your real name is quite commonplace or a little on the bland side – say, Jane Smith or Fred Jones. You need a name that's punchy and will stick in your readers' minds. It also needs to be distinctive enough to come up quickly on a search of Amazon books online, or Google. Type in Jane Smith or Fred Jones, and millions of them will come up! Be different, and think commercially.

Checking the availability of a name

It can be frustrating to hit upon what seems like a really great pen-name, only to find it's already been snapped up, or belongs to a famous personality such as an actor, musician or sportsperson you hadn't heard of. Google and other similar search engines are a quick and easy way to check the availability of your chosen pseudonym.

The gender issue

Are you a lady writer of thrillers? Think about your marketing, and whether you might want to write under a man's name. Why would you want to do this? Because it is a fact of publishing – in this age of post-feminism! – that most men will tend to buy thrillers written by men. Moreover, there is more of a thriller market for men than for women. 'Women's reads' often tend more to be the 'aga-saga' type, romance novels, historical novels with girls in shawls on the cover, or the female-orientated crime genre (e.g. Martina Cole). So you may find that even the punchiest and most commercial thriller will be compromised if it has a woman's name on the cover. Publishers are a wary bunch.

Lest this seem like a sexist conspiracy, remember that it cuts both ways: the bestselling romantic novelist, Emma Blair, is, in fact, a gentleman named Iain Blair writing under a female pseudonym.

And if you're a woman writer, don't worry about it one little bit. Play the game – get the book out there. The only potential problem is what you'll do later on should you ever be required to do publicity rounds or book-signings! These are issues you could discuss with your agent or publisher. If in doubt, one clever compromise is to sit on the fence and call yourself an androgynous name like 'Kim' or 'Alex', 'Sam', 'Sandy', 'Kerry', even 'Cameron' (think of the actress Cameron Diaz), to keep your gender a mystery until such time as your novel is successful enough for it not to matter. Or think of a catchy, different and unisex nickname: the brilliantly-named Twist Phelan is a successful lady author of legal thrillers.

Co-authorship

You may have written your novel with a partner, friend or colleague, and would ideally like to have both your names appear on the cover. This is more normal in the non-fiction world, but in fiction – and especially commercial fiction like the thriller genre – you will often find that publishers don't want two names on the cover. There are exceptions of course – such as Dustin Thomason and Ian Caldwell, authors of the bestseller *The Rule of Four*. But in general, that's how it is. Publishers have found that two names on the cover can confuse potential readers by giving the book the look of a non-fiction book. It can also clutter up the cover and spine too much, and won't draw the eye like a single fat, gold-lettered name.

Lots of names you might recognise and think of as single writers are really couples. Some, like 'John Case' (the husband-and-wife team Jim and Carolyn Hougan) are open about their true identity, while the real names of others are known only to their agents or publishers.

Choose your 'shared' name carefully. As I mentioned above, it may be wise – and publishers may urge you – to go for a male pseudonym as the Hougans did. Alternatively, one of the more androgynous ones above, such as Alex or Kim or Sandy, might suit you.

AGENTS – DO YOU NEED ONE?

The general consensus is that yes, you do. A literary agent is a professional specialist whose job it is to mediate between authors and publishers. A good agent will have all the right contacts within the publishing world, will know the best publishers to approach for different types and genres of writing, and will be able to negotiate the best deals when it comes to contract time. They work hard to represent authors' interests, and generally only ask for 15 per cent commission.

But getting an agent isn't easy – in fact it's probably no easier than getting a publisher. Agents, especially the top ones who represent famous writers, receive up to 300 unsolicited submissions every week. The rejection rate is enormous, partly because much of what they are sent is rubbish! Many writers fail to check that the agent of their choice even deals with their kind of book.

Some agents won't look at anything unless it's already highly polished and in publishable form. Others may be more flexible and take a writer on if they show promise, then work with them to get the novel ready to send out to publishers. This process may take months, and please note that by 'work with' I don't mean that the agent will do writing for you, or tell you what to write. Their input will generally be in the form of criticism. For some writers, this is their first major brush with hard criticism, and it may take some getting used to. But get used to it! If an agent has taken you on at all, there are a thousand authors out there who would kill to be in your shoes.

You should also be aware that having an agent, though it increases your chances of publication considerably, will not guarantee publication. Publishers will usually get round to reading the manuscript more quickly if it comes via an agent – especially one they've dealt with regularly – and they will generally have more respect for your work knowing that it's been 'vetted' by other professionals and deemed of publishable standard. But if it doesn't appeal sufficiently, or doesn't fit into their schedule, they may still reject it. Agents may have to trawl round quite a few publishers before one makes an offer on the book.

Quite a few writers get by very well without needing an agent. However, it's interesting to note that more and more publishers seem to be accepting only material submitted through an agent, especially at the more commercial end of the market and the realm of the thriller. This may be due to the fact that so many more people are trying to break into writing nowadays – it makes sense for publishers to want to use literary agencies as a 'filter' to sort out the wheat from the chaff and reduce the overwhelming quantity of submissions to a manageable level, whilst avoiding having to employ staff just to mail out rejections all day long! If this trend continues, we may eventually be seeing a time when writers will find it hard to get a publisher to even look at their work unless it comes through an agent.

APPROACHING A PUBLISHER DIRECT

If you decide to bypass agents and approach publishers direct, the first thing to check is that the publisher will actually look at work not submitted via a *bona fide* agent – as mentioned above, an increasing number won't.

The early approach

Some writers make their approach to publishers or agents *before* they've even completed the manuscript. In 1983, Robert Goddard kick-started his successful career by sending the first 50 pages of his debut novel *Past Caring* to Robert Hale. Based on this sample, the publisher asked to see more and eventually published the finished book.

The main advantage of making an early approach is the added incentive of knowing that someone is at least tentatively interested in your work. This makes the writing process much easier. However, there are also pitfalls. If a publisher or agent is impressed by the initial sample and asks to see more, there's the danger of dashing off the remainder of the book in too much of a hurry lest they lose interest, and turning in what amounts to little more than a first draft. Unless the writer is very lucky and the agent or publisher in question believes in them enough to work with them to improve the book, things may go no further and a very good opportunity wasted.

Approach the right people

Before you take the plunge and start sending material off for consideration, make sure that you're not wasting everyone's time by sending to the wrong agent or publisher. Inexperienced writers often earn black marks against their names by submitting completely inappropriate material. I know of one publisher specialising in fiction only, who is always receiving non-fiction submissions from writers! Needless to say, these receive no more than an exasperated sigh from the publisher, and are rejected automatically. Firing off at random like this is just a waste of everyone's time, not to mention money and paper.

Armed with a copy of *The Writer's Handbook* and/or using the lists given at the end of this book (see Appendix 3), do your research and identify the publishers or agents for whom your work would be most suited. Back this up by visiting your local bookshop or an online bookstore such as Amazon, checking out what books your chosen publisher has published, or what authors your chosen agent represents. Examine these books and authors in detail. Is this really the best possible niche for your work? A publisher who mostly produces chick-lit or detective novels, or an agent who represents Booker-type literary authors or poets, will probably not be the right people to approach with a hard-boiled thriller.

How many should I send out at a time?

You can send your samples to one agent or publisher at a time if desired. However it's usually more sensible to send out to a carefully-selected few, to put several hooks in the water at once. Before sending anything, make a final check on two points:

1. That they definitely are still handling your kind of book – things can change.

2. That their list is open, i.e. they are currently considering material from new authors.

All this takes is a quick phone call. A few seconds on the phone will potentially save you a lot of trouble, and avoid you waiting months only to receive a slip saying 'sorry, we don't deal with this kind of book', or 'sorry, our list is full at the moment'.

Have your lines prepared!

When you phone to check the above, you may just get through to a receptionist who will give you the basic information you need. But, depending on whom you're calling, you may find yourself talking to an actual agent or publisher. If they start asking you about your work, don't be caught unprepared. Jot down some notes before you call them, to enable you to describe your thriller concisely and interestingly. *'It's . . . well, kind of . . . you know . . . a bit like . . . sort of . . . hard to describe really . . .'* isn't going to win you any points.

WHAT TO SEND

You may be sitting on a complete and beautifully polished manuscript and be champing at the bit to show it off. Resist the temptation to send the whole thing out, as it's very bad form to do so unless specifically requested. The norm is to submit:

◆ The first three chapters

◆ A covering letter

◆ A synopsis

The covering letter

It's extremely important that the covering letter you send with your submission should 'pitch' your work effectively to agents or publishers. A pitch is simply a selling document, a snappy proposal designed to sum up your idea in a nutshell and get people excited about it. The ultimate pitch would take about five seconds to read, convince anyone who read it that they simply *must* snap you up before someone else does, and have them reaching for the phone in a hurry.

In practice, it takes a lot of hard thinking to condense your thriller into a hard-hitting pitch. This is a subject that whole creative writing workshops could be (and should be, but seldom are) devoted to. The main rules are:

◆ Keep it short and to the point – no waffle.

◆ Don't be aggressive or presumptuous (*'I'm sure you will agree this book is a sure-fire hit . . .'*).

◆ Explain as economically as possible what makes this book special and wildly different from its competitors, and why you think it would be popular.

◆ Show that you know the market and can compare your work to others'.

◆ Don't try to describe the plot and characters in the letter – leave that to the synopsis. The letter is just to introduce yourself and say why you think your work deserves their attention.

◆ Be confident and positive, but modest and polite.

◆ Don't be ingratiating or try to jump down the agent/ publisher's throat – remain professional and formal.

◆ Briefly outline a little about yourself, your writing experience, any previous publications, your goals and aspirations.

◆ If you have some interesting professional background that is relevant to your writing (e.g. if you are a criminal lawyer, ex-commando or former spy!), make sure they know about this.

As far as possible, try to find out the name of the most appropriate person to address your letter to, and what department or imprint they work for. Again, a quick call to the agency or publisher's receptionist will provide the relevant details.

Below is an example of how NOT to write to a publisher:

Dear Annie,

Enclosed is the full manuscript of my novel 'Rusty Nuts'. I know you only wanted the first three chapters, but I'm sure you'll enjoy it so much that you'll want to read the whole thing. All my friends and family say it's the best thriller they've ever read.

I chose your publishing company because I see you publish many of the big names, and I think I have a glittering career ahead of me. I've got lots more story ideas, and could send you those too – perhaps you could give me some advice on how I could pad them out into novels?

In the unlikely event that you don't want to publish my book, would you mind giving me a few tips on how I could improve it, and possibly some names of other publishers who might be interested? Please don't send me the usual form rejection slip! It's so impersonal. Writers are sensitive people with feelings – sometimes I think publishers get a kick out of undermining our creativity. Anyway, if you want to contact me, after five o'clock is best and my mobile number is 07677 123456789. Better still, I could pop over to your office during my lunch break?

I believe this project could be mutually profitable, and hope to hear from you a.s.a.p.

Yours,
A. Hopeful

P.S: What kind of advances do you pay? I got another angry letter from Barclaycard this morning.

The synopsis

Along with your letter you enclose a synopsis, which is a summary of the key points of the storyline, enough to give a full flavour of what your thriller is about but not too long. Try to keep it down to no more than two or three pages, double-spaced and easy to read.

As with the covering letter, make sure the synopsis is direct and exciting, and free of waffle – no need to go into the minute detail of every little sub-plot and character. Don't try to write your synopsis in a thriller-ish style that reflects the book itself – this isn't the blurb for the back cover! It should be written in simple, plain language, not too wordy. The synopsis should put across (but not necessarily in this order):

◆ The setting and background of the story.

◆ What real-life events, if any, have inspired it.

◆ The basic themes of the story (e.g. a tale of betrayal and corruption/intrigue and espionage).

◆ A brief description of the main characters, especially the hero/heroine: what they do, how they get involved in the story.

◆ The main events in the plot – what happens, who gets involved and how the characters are affected.

◆ What locations the story involves – are these glamorous and sexy? Gothic and spooky? Harsh and threatening?

◆ How the story resolves itself – happy ending? Dark ending? What becomes of the main characters?

PROFESSIONAL PRESENTATION OF YOUR MANUSCRIPT

You wouldn't dress in old rags to attend a job interview. Likewise, when you submit your work it should be as well-groomed and presentable as you can possibly make it. Some important rules are:

Hard copy only
Everything is done the old-fashioned, expensive way – on paper. Yes, it would be great if all agents and publishers accepted work by email or on CD, but for practical reasons (and their own protection against viruses and the like) they don't. Never try to email a submission unless you've specifically been told by the agent or publisher that it's permissible to do so.

Check the manuscript thoroughly before packing it up
Home printing machines sometimes go wrong with paper snarl-ups and so on, so check each page as it's printed and make sure they're all present and correct.

Use a decent quality of paper, plain white A4
Don't use that ultra-cheap copier paper that's too thin, almost like tracing paper, and avoid top-quality thick stuff that's too heavy to send in the post. Go for something in-between.

Keep it simple and clean
Don't bind the pages, and no fancy fonts or coloured paper as these gimmicks will not impress agents and publishers. No dog-eared pages, no finger-marks, no coffee stains!

Create a cover sheet
It should look something like this:

                                    Arthur McGee
                                 25 Nowhere Street
                               Fictionville, FN1 2AB
                                Tel: 01234 567890
                      Email: arthur@aspiringauthor.com

OUTCAST
by
JED SPRING
(Pseudonym of Arthur McGee)

                        Approx: 110,000 words

Numbering

Make sure each page of the manuscript is numbered, and include the title of the novel and your name in the upper left-hand corner of the header.

Re-printing

Don't keep using the same battered old rejected manuscript to send round to agents and publishers. Grit your teeth and re-print a fresh one each time. (Old manuscripts are generally useful for shopping lists and lining bird-cages, but not much else.) The extra cost will help focus the mind to ensure you send it to the right places!

Stationery

Never re-use old envelopes, as this looks shabby and tawdry. Package your work up in nice new padded envelopes, e.g. 'jiffy bags' or the bubble-wrap-lined ones you can get from post office shops.

Postage

Always include return postage with your work. This means buying extra envelopes and doubling your postage costs, but if you don't do it you might never hear back from the agent or publisher. Don't seal the envelope until you get to the post office. Have the package weighed *with* the return envelope folded inside, then have the appropriate postage put on the return envelope before sealing everything up. After a few repetitions of this ritual, postal staff may groan when they see you coming, so be very nice to them!

First-class postage

It's up to you whether to put first-class postage on both the outgoing and return envelopes – agents and publishers may take a while to get back to you, so second-class return postage won't cause any significant extra delay. However, first-class outgoing looks good and shows that you're keen!

Sending material abroad

The biggest thriller market in the world, by far, is the USA. If you live in the UK or Europe you may be tempted to submit work to US agents or publishers. This can be expensive, especially if the agent or publisher wants to see an entire manuscript and you have to send a chunky package. You will also need to include the appropriate IRCs (international reply coupons) by way of return postage. IRCs can be obtained at your main post office.

America is rather more email-savvy than the UK, and some US agents do accept submissions electronically. However, always check first that this is the case, and ensure that your attachments are 100 per cent virus-free.

THE WAITING GAME

Sometimes it seems like all a writer ever does is wait around for things to happen! As a profession we are very dependent on 'that' email or 'that' phone call from the agent or publisher to tell us what's happening with our work. You're always waiting for *something* – to hear if you've been accepted, to know what changes need making to the manuscript, to know if the contract's come through, to know publication dates, see what your cover looks like, see how much money you're getting, and on it goes! But the longest and most frustrating wait is that of the unknown, un-published writer who's just sent out their pitch and sample to the agent or publisher (or selection of agents and publishers) of their choice for the first time. Now the hook is in the water, you have no choice but to sit around and wait to see if the fish are biting.

All I can say of this period of your life is: try not to let it get to you too much. It might be a long haul – three, even four months sometimes. With so many budding writers out there, response times are steadily lengthening. True, if your project is really hot they may get back to you very much sooner than that. But don't get into the negative habit of expecting good news in the mail from day to day. If you do, you court cruel disappointment. Try to be detached, and prepare yourself for rejection. I don't say this to be pessimistic, but the possibility of rejection is a reality that haunts each and every stage of the process, and the higher you climb the further there is to fall!

But do hold this thought – that ONE day you WILL get that reply telling you that your work is accepted. If you have ability and are prepared to develop it, if you have what it takes to see it through, you WILL be a writer. And that is a moment of unparalleled triumph in your life that is surely worth waiting for.

Don't be a pest!
No matter how frustrated you may be feeling, never phone and pester the agent or publisher with demands of '*Well,*

have you read it yet?'. You might be the next Dan Brown, but if they think you're going to be a pest you may well put them off you. Remember, they can afford to be extremely choosy.

COPING WITH REJECTION AND CRITICISM

Getting into this business unprepared for taking rejection and criticism is like a novice boxer climbing into the ring unprepared for being punched. Get used to the idea. Like the boxer, you're going to take a beating; and like him, you have to learn how to take the knocks. Don't give up – in this business, persistence most definitely pays. Many successful authors endured scores or even hundreds of rejections before even getting published. If you believe in yourself, you owe it to yourself to keep going. Take inspiration from the words of thriller writer J.A. Konrath: 'There's a word for writers who don't give up. It's called *published.*'

You can be rejected for a number of reasons.

◆ Your writing skills still need a little sharpening; this doesn't mean your idea is no good, just that you could do it more justice.

◆ The publisher or agent's list is full and you didn't check!

◆ The publisher may simply be so snowed under with unsolicited material that it had to close its doors – no reflection on your work but simply a reality of the business.

◆ A publisher may have recently brought out a thriller similar to yours.

◆ The publisher may be wrong! Remember that, as with all the arts, publishing is a subjective business. One agent's reader I know turned away an author because they didn't like his book, thinking it was too violent. The author took his work to another agent, promptly got taken on and quickly became a very famous name who made a lot of money for all concerned. The agent's reader who had rejected him was not too popular with their boss.

Revenge is sweet . . .

But not smart. Some rejected writers vent their spleen by sending sarcastic or vindictive letters to agents or publishers, telling them how stupid they were to turn down such brilliant material. Writing nasty letters can be great therapy, but earning a bad reputation among publishing professionals is not going to do your writing career any good. As rock star, Ozzy Osborne, once said: 'Don't mess anyone around on your way up . . . cause you might need them when you're on your way down!'

'Positive rejections'

If a publisher or agent rejects you but makes some sort of critical observation, e.g. 'this showed quality but in the end we decided it wasn't for us' or 'you write well but we felt your characters were a little underdeveloped', take it as a good sign. These busy professionals don't have time to make individual comments on every piece of work they turn away. *Listen to their advice and keep trying.* Don't re-send to the same company, however: unfortunately once they reject you, that chance is gone.

If they want you . . .

A positive response from a publisher or agent can be something of a left-handed compliment. Even after your work is noticed by an agent or publisher who believes it has potential, you won't be exempt from hard criticism. Here is a sample of what a report from an agent or editor might look like:

p. 57: This is silly.

p. 69: Romantic scene very corny.

p. 73: Reconsider rewriting the end of this chapter – poor ending.

p. 81: Cliché

p. 86: This character is just not believable.

p. 95: There's very little tension here.

p. 96: This scene could be drawn out more, very rushed.

p. 101: Last line – poor writing, a bit schoolboyish.

p. 104: Seems a bit far-fetched.

p. 109: Nobody's going to believe your character would act this way: goes against psychology.

p.110: Boring! If you're going to bother with a bit of background detail it needs to be well-done and interesting.

p. 112: Storyline is getting stale at this point. Consider inserting a whole new plot twist.

p. 117: This is just too coincidental.

p. 121: This character seems a little underdeveloped. It might be good to have a little more background.

p. 127: Rather poor writing here.

p. 131: I don't think that this quite ties up.

p. 139: This is very disappointing. A crucial moment in the story, glossed over in a few scanty lines.

p. 146: 'he somehow escaped' – lazy writing.

p. 148: Last 2 paras are trashy – need redoing.

p. 152: This whole sequence lacks suspense.

p. 157: I still think this dialogue is awful.

p. 160: Character seems schizophrenic, veering from one emotion to another.

p. 167: Needs more tension . . . whole passage very dull, characters feel about to fall asleep.

And be ready to receive criticism at all levels. Even after you've cleared the twin hurdles of securing an agent and getting a publisher interested, you won't necessarily be out of the woods. You may be told that a scene, or a character, or even a whole aspect of the plot, isn't working and requires a rewrite – or sometimes, quite extensive surgery. There may be clear reasons given to you as to why it 'isn't working', for instance it may be too unbelievable. Other times there won't.

How do you respond to criticism?

Grouch and groan? By all means, but do it privately. This is a defining moment in your life. You can either define the moment by getting on with the job of doing the necessary rewrites; or you can *let the moment define you* by showing the editor or agent what kind of a sulky, unprofessional prima donna they're really working with!

Grumble by all means – take it out on a punch-bag, kick a tin can all down the street, rant and rage at the sky. But don't, *whatever you do*, rant and rage at the agent or publisher. These folks want to form professional and productive long-term relationships with writers. They're trying to help you sell your work and make some money so you can go on writing more – and so that maybe one day writing will become a full-time living for you. The very fact that they're even bothering to take the time to criticise you is evidence that, slowly, you're nearing your goal.

Ask yourself who you'd rather be – the unpublished author who chose art over reality (get in line – there are millions); or a published author with a good career ahead of them? So what if you had to sacrifice an idea you liked, chop out a scene, even lose a favourite character? They still exist, and you can always reuse them later, when you've written more and have that bit more authority to control what goes into your books.

SELF-PUBLISHING AND WHY YOU SHOULD AVOID IT

For writers who have given up trying to get published through the normal channels, there is a whole industry set up to tempt them into paying for their own publication. These self-publishing companies advertise everywhere, even in reputable writers' journals (who should really be keeping them out).

But don't do it. Especially in the realm of commercial fiction, and with very, very few exceptions, self-publishing is rightly considered as *phoney* publishing. This is mainly because there is absolutely no quality control involved. A self-published novel has as much intrinsic value as a fake degree or doctorate purchased from a spurious college or self-styled university – zero. Nobody will ever take your book seriously, no writers' organisation worth its salt will allow you to become a member, and your work will most likely disappear without trace very quickly as you will have no chance of competing with 'the big boys'. There is every chance that all you'll be left with is a house full of thousands of books that you can't get rid of. Your local writers' group may admire your achievement, but 'real' writers (which is what you wanted to be, remember?) will sneer.

Worse, a good run of decently-produced books may set you back £10,000 or more. If you're going to spend that kind of money on launching a writing career, do yourself a favour and spend it on buying as many good books as you can on the subject, or attending courses and workshops given by commercially-published writers with good advice to offer. Best of all, use that money to take some time out, sit down and write.

If your thriller novel has done the rounds of every agent and publisher under the sun and still fails to win their enthusiasm, before you take the plunge into self-publishing maybe you should step back and accept that it just wasn't good enough. You might be a great storyteller with real talent, but your book just wasn't right for the market. It's tough, but don't make it tougher on yourself by throwing money away on the self-publishing industry.

STRIKING THE DEAL

To the first-time author, getting a publishing contract is the equivalent of finding the Holy Grail, accompanied by choirs of angels and a fanfare of heavenly trumpets. But don't get too dreamy yet. Make sure the contract is something you actually want to sign. Remember it's a legally binding document. Some contracts are single-page affairs, while others are quite a few pages long and burrow deep into legal detail. Read them very carefully indeed.

Two important things you shouldn't sign away are:

1. **Money** – check the small print for clauses like 'the author agrees to contribute the sum of (£££) towards publishing costs'. The main use for such contracts is to light fires with.

2. **Copyright** – authors should always retain copyright, or legal ownership, of anything they write. Giving it away means that it simply isn't yours any more. You could be kicking yourself for the rest of your life if you signed away for a few pounds a property that went on to make millions for someone else!

If you've managed to get yourself a *bona fide* literary agent, they will read the contract through for you and make sure the terms are to your best advantage. They may even be able to push the publisher for better terms, although many publishers won't be pushed very far. If you haven't got an agent, it may be very prudent to join an organisation like the Society of Authors, who will vet your contract and advise you accordingly.

If a contract isn't to your advantage, have the courage to walk away from it. Keep trying elsewhere – talent will out eventually.

MONEY

Payment for authors comes in two basic forms: advances and royalties.

Advances

The advance is the first money you'll see from the novel, and the amount can vary hugely – the very best agents with the right contacts can whip up publishers' expectations to the tune of £100,000 or even more. However this only happens occasionally! Most advances are very much smaller, and some are very small indeed. Getting a small advance doesn't necessarily mean that your book won't do well. Many best-selling authors started out with modest advances, and then went on to sell (and make) millions.

Royalties

Royalties are payments based on sales of the book, usually between 10–15 per cent of the retail price but climbing to up as much as 50 per cent for foreign language editions (which for many bestselling authors is where the real money is). You only start to see royalties once you've 'paid off' your advance. One consolation if you only received a small advance is that, assuming the book sells, you'll at least start to see royalties quite quickly. Royalties are usually paid twice a year.

Subsidiary rights

In addition to royalties earned from sales of the book in their home market, authors can earn money from a whole range of subsidiary rights. One of the most coveted of these has always been the US rights, as the American market can be huge for the right book. Other subsidiary rights that can generate income for the writer include film and television rights, translation rights, serial rights for newspapers and magazines, audio book rights, and, for the seriously successful thriller, even such things as computer game adaptations. This is where a good agent, with a canny understanding of the publishing market, can be a great asset.

Writers and tax

Tax, like wasps, is an unavoidable evil. A writer comes under the same category as any other self-employed person, and if you make any income from your writing the taxman will want to get his share of all your profits. Your profit is anything left over from your writing income after deducting allowable expenses. Keep simple accounts, making note of anything you buy for your writing:

◆ Books, paper, computer equipment are all tax-deductible.

◆ If you rent a room to write in or use part of your house as an office, you can include the relevant gas, electricity and telephone expenses.

◆ You can include research costs as a tax deduction, and certain travel expenses. (Don't get carried away, though, as the tax-man may not agree that your three weeks in Barbados with the whole family counts as a genuine research trip!)

PROMOTION OF THE BOOK

From the moment a deal is signed, publishers will be pulling out the stops to maximise their sales. However, even bestselling authors are expected to help in the process of publicising a book and helping with marketing ideas.

There are many things a writer can do to help promote a book. *Before* the book comes out you can:

◆ Form a good relationship with the publicity/marketing department at your publishing house, to help them form an effective campaign.

◆ Make sure local bookstores know about the forthcoming publication of your book.

◆ Find out what local colleges offer courses in writing, and make sure they know who you are.

◆ Make contact with local reading and writers' groups.

◆ Find out what literary festivals are coming up – see if you can get involved.

After the book comes out, you can press on even harder:

Book launch
Launch the book aggressively by organising events and inviting the media. Your publisher may also organise publicity, and you should get as involved as possible.

Media interest
If your book is about something unusual, that in itself could generate media interest. Explore the avenues. What other books, or films, can you align yours with to create interest?

Local bookstores

Get friendly with your local bookstore – you may be able to do a talk there to help promote interest in your book. A book signing by a local author often draws quite a crowd to the bookstore, which will go down well with them.

Talks

If you're confident with public speaking, get yourself invited to do some talks. Social clubs such as the golf club, Women's Institute, Rotary club, etc., often invite after-dinner speakers to talk about interesting subjects. People are quite fascinated by the process of writing a book, and will be interested to hear your personal experience. Read out exciting passages from the book, to tempt people to buy it!

Colleges

Do the rounds of colleges to give talks. Find out what universities nearby offer courses on creative writing: they will be interested to hear from a writer who has actually made it into commercial publishing.

Radio and TV

Approach local radio and television. One professional author I spoke to offers a free copy of her book as a competition prize in exchange for 15 minutes' air time talking about her work.

Reviews

When friends rave about your book, thank them sincerely but suggest they rave on Amazon! Enthusiastic reviews sell books.

Authors' websites

More and more published authors, big and small, have their own websites. The website is the centre of your operation, a place you can quickly refer people for information about you and your work. A good website is an excellent calling card. As your name (or pseudonym) starts to get around, publishers and the press may visit it, potentially leading to requests for more books, articles or interviews. Your website is available to be viewed 24 hours a day, every day of the year, by anyone in the world – it's the advertising helper that never sleeps.

You can have links from your site to online bookstores such as Amazon, if your book is available there (which most books are). You can also have links to other organisations, such as International Thriller Writers (membership open to all commercially-published thriller authors).

Workshop for Chapter 8

➢ Every time you read a thriller novel, try to imagine how you would condense the story into a tight and interesting pitch. What were the key elements that would grab the attention of an agent or publisher?

➢ Practise writing synopses and covering letters, 'rehearsing' them before you send anything off. Think of these as pieces of creative writing in their own right –

hone and perfect them until they convey just the right tone and impact to give your work the best possible presentation.

➤ Make sure you are well armed with all the information you need to make the best approaches to publishers and/or agents. If you haven't already done so, obtain a copy of The Writer's Handbook (see Appendix 1).

➤ Visit the websites of published thriller authors and see how they have presented themselves/promoted their work. Think about the things that make you and your work interesting, and how best they could be put across in your own website.

AN EXCLUSIVE INTERVIEW WITH LEE CHILD

In the course of writing this book I was very honoured to have the opportunity to conduct the following interview with top thriller writer, Lee Child, author of the bestselling Jack Reacher series.

SM: What would you say are the necessary key elements for a great thriller?
LC: I'd say there are two important elements: characters and story structure. Obviously we have to care about the characters in order to worry about their fate, but more than that, we need at least the main character to rise toward the heroic or mythic in terms of 'size'. Similarly, the story should contain elements of struggle and challenge similar to the great myths of the past. There's a reason that myths survive: it's because, deep down, we need them to.

SM: Where do you get your ideas and inspiration for your own books?
LC: Pretty much everywhere. Every day the newspaper carries about five stories that would make great thriller

fiction. The real difficulty is the opposite to what most people imagine: not, 'Can I come up with an idea?' but, 'Which of these many ideas should I invest a year's work in?'

SM: What advice would you have for aspiring writers trying to break into this genre?
LC: Put simply, my advice is ignore all advice. If you've been reading for years, you're ready. Just go ahead and write exactly the book you want to read – even if you're sure everyone else in the world is going to hate it. Because they won't – if it's written with passion and vitality, lots of other people will respond. If it's written with one eye on what the 'market' is doing, it'll be constricted and cardboard and inorganic.

Glossary

Advance: Variable sum of money paid by the publisher to the author in advance of royalties, usually on signing of the publishing contract.

Agency agreement: A contract between the author and literary agent, giving details of their mutual responsibilities.

Agent: (or Literary agent) Publishing professional who acts on an author's behalf and negotiates contracts, etc., for a percentage of the author's royalties (usually 10–15 per cent).

Agent's reader: The person employed by the literary agency to assess the suitability of a piece of writing.

Allowable expenses: Business expenses that an author can offset against tax, e.g. paper and ink, computer equipment, books and other research material, travelling expenses.

Antagonist: A character who goes against the protagonist (see **Baddie**).

Antonym: A word that means the opposite of another.

Audio-book: A novel recorded on tape or CD for listening purposes.

Baddie: A villainous character in a story, against whom main characters struggle.

Best-seller: Very popular book that enters the best-seller lists.

Blockbuster: A smash-hit; also a 'summer read' aimed at the holiday market, often a long novel of over 500 pages.

Blurb: Short write-up on the back cover that summarises the plot and attracts prospective readers.

Book fair: Trade event attended by publishers, literary agents and authors to promote new books and make deals.

Book-signing: Usually taking place at a bookstore, publicity event where a visiting author meets readers and signs copies of their book.

Category fiction: A specific genre of book such as a romantic novel, western, thriller, detective story, etc.

Cliff-hanger: A moment of great suspense in a story, often at the end of a chapter, which acts to tease the reader and keep them turning the pages.

Complimentary copies: Quantity of free copies given out to the author by the publisher when a book first comes out, often used for promotional purposes.

Continuity: The sequence of plot points in a story; the need to maintain a consistent and logical storyline.

Contract: A document that describes the arrangement between a publisher and author, giving details of subsidiary rights, financial arrangements, etc. Once signed the document is legally binding.

Copy: Term meaning either a copy of a book, or a piece of text sent to an editor or agent.

Copyright: The legal rights that an author has to prevent others from copying their work or passing it off as their own.

Cover sheet: Title page that the author creates for their manuscript, giving the title of the novel as well as their name, pseudonym and contact details.

Deadline: Date by which a manuscript is to be completed sent to the publisher.

Description: A passage that portrays a scene, the appearance of a place or person.

Dialogue: The words spoken by characters, distinguished from the rest of the text by inverted commas.

Draft: An initial version of the story, often in need of extensive revision.

Editor: An important member of the publisher's staff, who makes decisions regarding the suitability of a manuscript and may suggest changes to it.

Film option: A legal arrangement giving a production company the right to base a film on a novel.

Flashback: Narrative device allowing the reader to travel back in time or in the memory of a character.

Font: A style and size of typeface, e.g. Times New Roman 12.

Genre: A category into which a book falls, e.g. historical novel, romantic novel, thriller, sci-fi, etc.

Grabber: A powerful opening to a book that makes the reader want to keep reading.

Hack: Derogatory (but fairly humorous!) term for a jobbing writer who may be just doing it for the money.

Hardcopy: A paper printout of part or all of a manuscript.

Hardback: A book produced with a stiff cover, usually in a slightly larger format than the paperback edition.

Header: The upper margin of a page, showing the title of the novel and author's name.

Imprint: A sub-company within of a large publishing group, e.g. Bantam is an imprint of Transworld.

IRC: International Reply Coupon, used in lieu of postage for sending material overseas (usually to the USA).

Libel: Publishing a damaging statement against a person's name or reputation, possibly leading to a legal dispute.

Manuscript: The text of the novel before it is published in book form.

Market: A place where a book is sold; a potential readership for a book.

MS: Abbreviated term meaning 'manuscript', often used in correspondence with publishers and agents.

Page-turner: A book that is exciting to read: 'it's a real page-turner'; a narrative device such as a cliff-hanger that encourages the reader to keep turning the pages.

Paperback: A popular mass-market edition of a book in pocket-sized format with a flexible card jacket.

Paperback rights: The legal right to bring out a title in paperback, often sold by one publisher to another.

Pitch: The sales talk that an author or agent uses to promote the publication of a book.

Plagiarism: The illegal act of copying another writer's work, claiming it as one's own.

Plot: The shape, structure and direction of a storyline.

Proofs: The typeset print-out of a book, ready for final checking before it goes to the printers.

Proofreading: A last check through the manuscript to fix any errors before publication.

Protagonist: A leading character in a story, sometimes the 'I' character through whom the reader views the action.

Pseudonym: The pen-name that an author can choose to appear instead of their real name on the cover of the book.

Public lending right: A small sum of money that an author receives each time a book of theirs is borrowed from a library.

Publishing credit: A record of a published work that a writer can add to their CV.

Readership: The audience for a particular book or genre of book; a body of fans built up by a popular author.

Reading fee: Sum of money charged by some (relatively few) literary agents to read and assess a manuscript, a practice often frowned upon by authors as well as other agents.

Rejection: A letter or form slip sent back with a returned manuscript, telling the writer their submission has not been successful; something you tear to pieces and stamp into the ground!

Research: The important process of gathering facts and background details as preparation for writing a novel.

Review: An appraisal of a book by a critic or journalist, published in a literary review, newspaper or magazine.

Rewrites: The process of revising the first draft of a novel, often making extensive changes, deletions and additions. The novel may go into several drafts before completion.

Royalties: Payments made to the author, usually six-monthly, on the basis of sales. If the author has an agent, the money is paid to them and then passed on to the author minus the agency's commission.

SAE: A stamped, self-addressed envelope, vitally important to include with manuscript submissions.

Scene: A passage of writing depicting an event, piece of action or dialogue. Scenes can be short and there can be several within a chapter.

Self-publishing: When authors pay from their own pocket to have a book produced.

Setting: The time and place in which a story is based.

Slush pile: The 'graveyard' of the publisher's office, where unsolicited manuscripts pile up and may never get any further.

Sub-genre: A specialised type-within-a-type of book, for example the espionage thriller or the 'Grail' thriller popularised by *The Da Vinci Code*.

Submission: A piece of work sent by a hopeful writer to an agent or publisher.

Sub-plot: A strand of the storyline woven around, and adding an extra dimension to, the main story.

Subsidiary rights: The various rights, other than UK book publishing rights, that can be sold to create new markets for a property. These may include film and TV rights, comic book and computer games, audio books, serialisation, and foreign language rights.

Suspense: The building up of anticipatory tension in the reader; the sense of urgency generated by an uncertain outcome or perilous situation.

Synonym: A word meaning the same as another word.

Synopsis: A condensed run-down of the plot of a novel, used to give agents and publishers a quick idea of what the novel is about.

Theme: A concept or idea running through a story.

Thesaurus: A useful reference book offering ideas on synonyms and wording.

Title auction: When publishers bid against each other for a 'hot' property, often stirred up by a skilful literary agent who aims to drive the price up as high as possible.

Twist: A sudden event in a plot that takes the reader by surprise, adds an unexpected new element to the story or sends it off in a different direction.

Typesetting: The process of setting up the way a book will appear when printed.

Typo: A term for a typing or spelling error in the manuscript, which is hopefully spotted during proofreading.

Unsolicited script: A manuscript (or sample of a manuscript) sent to an agent or publisher on spec, without invitation. It is generally bad form to send a complete manuscript unless requested to do so.

Viewpoint: The 'eyes' through which the reader views the telling of the story, e.g. first person, or third person.

Voice: The distinctive personal style that authors strive to develop.

Wordage: The approximate number of words (rounded up or down to the nearest 1000) contained in a manuscript. This is easily calculated on a computer, and the number should be included with the submission to give an idea of the length of the complete ms.

Writer's block: The inability to come up with ideas; being 'stuck', often in the middle of the book-writing process and perhaps due to mental fatigue or a loss of motivation.

Writers' circle or group: A group of writers meeting informally, usually once a month, to share and discuss their work-in-progress.

Writing seminar or workshop: A more guided event than a writers' circle meeting, where one or more published authors give talks or offer guidance to writers, and where writers can meet and share ideas.

Appendix 1

USEFUL BOOKS AND PUBLICATIONS

The following are a just a handful of the many titles that can be helpful for writers, offering education and inspiration (and sometimes both).

On writing and publishing:

- *Dictionary of Printing and Publishing* (Peter Collin Publishing)
- *Give 'Em What they Want* Blythe Camenson and Marshall J Cook (Writers' Digest Books)
- *How to Get Published and Make a Lot of Money* Susan Page (Piatkus)
- *How to Write a Blockbuster* Sarah Harrison (Allison & Busby)
- *How to Write and Sell a Synopsis* Stella Whitelaw (Allison & Busby)
- *How to Write and Sell your First Novel* Oscar Collier with Frances Spatz-Leighton (Writers' Digest Books)
- *How to Write Damn Good Fiction* James Frey (Macmillan)
- *Lessons from a Lifetime of Writing* David Morrell (Writers' Digest Books)
- *On Writing* Stephen King (New English Library) (Hodder & Stoughton)

- *Plotting the Novel* Michael Legat (Robert Hale)
- *Publishing a Book* Robert Spicer (How To Books)
- *Researching for Writers* Marion Field (How To Books)
- *The Beginner's Guide to Writing a Novel* Marina Oliver (How To Books)
- *The Writer's Rights* Michael Legat (A. & C. Black)
- *Writer's Guide to Getting Published* Chriss McCallum (How To Books)
- *Writing for Pleasure and Profit* Michael Legat (Robert Hale)

Grammar and use of English

- *English Dictionary for Students* (Peter Collin Publishing)
- *Oxford Dictionary of English Grammar* (Oxford University Press)
- *Oxford Everyday Grammar* (Oxford University Press)
- *Oxford Guide to Plain English* (Oxford University Press)
- *Teach Yourself English Grammar* (Hodder & Stoughton)
- *The Elements of Style* William Strunk Jr. and E. B. White (Macmillan Publishing Co, New York)
- *The Nuts and Bolts of Writing* Michael Legat (Robert Hale)
- *Vocabulary for English* (Peter Collin Publishing)
- *Write Tight* William Brohaugh (Writer's Digest)

The Writer's Handbook

No UK-based writer should really be without the 'yellow bible', *The Writer's Handbook*. This hefty volume is updated annually and contains listings of all the main publishers and literary agents in the UK and Ireland, as well as many in the USA. It also features many articles of interest to writers, dealing with topics such as taxation, copyright, contracts, and so on. The Handbook also provides lists of writing courses, writers' groups and other useful associations. For those interested in screenwriting, there are also contact details for film and TV production companies. *The Writer's Handbook* is a great investment at around £15.00 a year, and is available from all good bookshops.

Other books of interest

Writing thrillers is more than just about writing – it's about storytelling generally, and you should try to read as much about the wider subject as possible. The first two books on this list offer fascinating insights into the mind of one of the greatest storytellers of them all, Alfred Hitchcock. If you can get hold of it, film director Francois Truffaut's study of the great man's work is a compelling read and crammed with exclusive interviews.

- *Hitchcock on Hitchcock* edited by Stanley Gottlieb (Faber & Faber)
- *Hitchcock: The Definitive Study* François Truffaut (Paladin)
- *Danse Macabre* Stephen King (Warner Books)

Stephen King is one of the great writers of our time, and *Danse Macabre* is a fascinating study of several decades of the horror and thriller genre in literature, film and television, told in King's inimitable style. More academic than you might expect, and very rewarding for anyone interested in writing.

Other publications

Writing Magazine
First Floor,
Victoria House,
143–144 The Headrow,
Leeds LS1 5RL
Tel: 0113 200 2929
Website: www.writersnews.co.uk

Writers' Forum
PO Box 3229,
Bournemouth BH1 1ZS
Tel: 01202 589 828
Email: editorial@writers-forum.com
Website: www.worldwidewriters.com

The New Writer
PO Box 60,
Cranbrook,
Kent TN17 2ZR
Tel: 01580 212 626
Email: editor@thenewwriter.com
Website: www.thenewwriter.com

Appendix 2

THRILLERS TO READ AND SEE

More than anything, you should be immersing yourself in thrillers themselves. The following list of 20 novels and 20 movies is very far from complete, but represent a handful of examples of the genre that are worth looking at. Of the films listed below, a number are adapted from novels, e.g. *The Bourne Identity* (Robert Ludlum) and *A Time to Kill* (John Grisham).

Books to read

- *Creepers* — David Morrell (Headline)
- *Cross Current* — Christine Kling (Robert Hale)
- *Die Trying* — Lee Child (Bantam)
- *Firestarter* — Stephen King (Hodder)
- *First to Die* — James Patterson (Headline)
- *Get Shorty* — Elmore Leonard (Phoenix)
- *Last Light* — Andy McNab (Corgi)
- *Last Man Standing* — David Baldacci (Pocket)
- *Midnight Runner* — Jack Higgins (HarperCollins)
- *Persuader* — Lee Child (Bantam)
- *Pronto* — Elmore Leonard (Phoenix)
- *Spurred Ambition* — Twist Phelan (Robert Hale)
- *The Blood Partnership* — Seth Garner (Robert Hale)

- *The Brotherhood of the Rose* — David Morrell (Headline)
- *The Da Vinci Code* — Dan Brown (Corgi)
- *The Dead Zone* — Stephen King (Hodder)
- *The Eighth Day* — John Case (Arrow)
- *The Firm* — John Grisham (Hodder)
- *The Last Spymaster* — Gayle Lynds (St Martin's Press)
- *The Templar Legacy* — Steve Berry (Hodder)

Movies to watch

- *A History of Violence* — Dir. David Cronenberg
- *A Time to Kill* — Dir. Joel Schumacher
- *Absolute Power* — Dir. Clint Eastwood
- *Dark Blue* — Dir. Curtis Hanson
- *Deep Red* — Dir. Dario Argento
- *Duel* — Dir. Steven Spielberg
- *Executive Decision* — Dir. Stuart Baird
- *For Your Eyes Only* — Dir. John Glen
- *L.A. Confidential* — Dir. Curtis Hanson
- *Man on Fire* — Dir. Tony Scott
- *North by Northwest* — Dir. Alfred Hitchcock
- *Notorious* — Dir. Alfred Hitchcock
- *Proof of Life* — Dir. Taylor Hackford
- *Ransom* — Dir. Ron Howard
- *Ronin* — Dir. John Frankenheimer
- *Spy Games* — Dir. Tony Scott
- *The Abyss* — Dir. James Cameron
- *The Bourne Identity* (remake) — Dir. Doug Liman
- *The Conversation* — Dir. Francis Ford Coppola
- *Three Days of the Condor* — Dir. Sydney Pollack

Appendix 3

UK LITERARY AGENTS AND PUBLISHERS

The following list of agents and publishers all handle commercial thrillers. Before submitting anything to any of these, or to any other, give them a quick call to double-check that this is still the case.

Agents

◆ **Anubis Literary Agency**, 6 Birdhaven Close, Lighthorne, Warwick CV35 0BE, Tel: 01926 642 588

◆ **Conville & Walsh Ltd**, 2 Ganton Street, London W1F 7QL, Tel: 020 7287 3030

◆ **Darley Anderson Literary, TV and Film Agency**, Estelle House, 11 Eustace Road, London SW6 1JB, Tel: 020 7385 6652

◆ **David Grossman Literary Agency Ltd**, 118b Holland Park Avenue, London W11 4UA, Tel: 020 7221 2770

◆ **David O'Leary Literary Agents**, 10 Landsdowne Court, Landsdowne Rise, London W11 2NR, Tel: 020 7229 1623

◆ **Dorian Literary Agency**, Upper Thornehill, 27 Church Road, Saint Marychurch, Torquay TQ1 4QY, Tel: 01803 312 095

◆ **Dorie Simmonds Agency**, 67 Upper Berkeley Street, London W1H 7QX, Tel: 020 7569 8686

◆ **Ed Victor Ltd**, 6 Bailey Street, Bedford Square, London WC1B 3HE, Tel: 020 7304 4100

◆ **Gregory & Company, Authors' Agents**, 3 Barb Mews, London W6 7PA, Tel: 020 7610 4676

◆ **International Scripts**, 1a Kidbrooke Park Road, London SE3 0LR, Tel: 020 8319 8666

◆ **Jane Judd Literary Agency**, 18 Belitha Villas, London N1 1PD, Tel: 020 7607 0273

◆ **Luigi Bonomi Associates Ltd**, 91 Great Russell Street, London WC1B 3PS, Tel: 020 7637 1234

◆ **Peters, Fraser and Dunlop (PFD) Ltd**, Drury House, 34–43 Russell Street, London WC2B 5HA, Tel: 020 7344 1000

◆ **Pollinger Limited**, 9 Staple Inn, London WC1V 7QH, Tel: 020 7404 0342

◆ **Sheil Land Associates Ltd**, 53 Doughty Street, London WC1N 2LS, Tel: 020 7405 9351

◆ **Teresa Chris Literary Agency Ltd**, 43 Mussard Road, London W6 8NR, Tel: 020 7386 0633

◆ **The Ampersand Agency**, Ryman's Cottages, Little Tew, OX7 4JJ, Tel: 01608 683 677

◆ **Watson Little Ltd**, Capo Di Monte, Windmill Hill, London NW3 6RJ, Tel: 020 7431 0770

Publishers

As larger publishing houses continue to get larger by gobbling up smaller ones, be aware that some of the larger publishers listed below, e.g. Random House, have a range of *imprints* or sub-companies who deal with different types of books and essentially operate as independent companies. For fuller details of these, as well as for contact names, consult your yellow bible, *The Writer's Handbook*.

- **Robert Hale Ltd**, Clerkenwell House, 45–47 Clerkenwell Green, London EC1R 0HT, Tel: 020 7251 2661
- **Harlequin Mills & Boon (Mira Books),** Eton House, 18–24 Paradise Road, Richmond, Surrey TW9 1SR, Tel: 020 8288 2800
- **HarperCollins**, 77–85 Fulham Palace Road, Hammersmith, London W6 8JB, Tel: 020 8741 7070
- **Hodder Headline**, 338 Euston Road, London NW1 3BH, Tel: 020 7873 6000
- **Macmillan Publishers Ltd**, The Macmillan Building, 4 Crinian Street, London N1 9XW, Tel: 020 7833 4000
- **The Orion Publishing Group Ltd**, Orion House, 5 Upper St Martins Lane, London WC2H 9EA, Tel: 020 7240 3444
- **Penguin UK**, 80 Strand, London WC2R 0RL, Tel: 020 7010 3000
- **Piatkus Books**, 5 Windmill Street, London W1T 2JA, Tel: 020 7631 0710
- **Random House Group Ltd**, 20 Vauxhall Bridge Road, London SW1V 2SA, Tel: 020 7840 8400
- **Severn House Publishers**, 9–15 High Street, Sutton, Surrey SM1 1DF, Tel: 020 8770 3930
- **Simon and Schuster**, Africa House, 74–78 Kingsway, London WC2B 6AH, Tel: 020 7316 1900
- **Souvenir Press Ltd**, 43 Great Russell Street, London WC1B 3PA, Tel: 020 7580 9307/8 or 020 7637 5711
- **Time Warner Books UK**, Brettenham House, Lancaster Place, London WC2E 7EN, Tel: 020 7911 8000
- **Transworld Publishers Ltd**, 61–63 Uxbridge Road, London W5 5SA, Tel: 020 8579 2652
- **Twenty-first Century Publishers Ltd**, Braunton Barn, Kiln Lane, Isfield TN22 5UE, Tel: 01892 522802

WRITERS' ORGANISATIONS

International Thriller Writers, Inc (ITW)
PO Box 311,
Eureka, CA 95502,
USA
Website: www.internationalthrillerwriters.com
Co-Presidents: David Morrell and Gayle Lynds

ITW is the only organisation I know of in the world that exists exclusively and specifically to promote the thriller genre. In less than two years since its foundation by some of the world's biggest names in thriller-writing, ITW has gathered over 400 members with a cumulative profile showing a stunning 1.7 billion copies sold worldwide. Members include top authors Lee Child, David Morrell, Faye Kellerman and David Baldacci. To qualify for membership, you must be the author of a thriller published by a ITW-approved commercial publisher. A list of these is to be found on the ITW website.

ITW produces a popular online newsletter, The Thriller Readers Newsletter, to which non-members can subscribe. This is filled with information on new releases, reviews, author interviews, thriller events and anything pertaining to the genre. Subscription to the newsletter is free – visit website: www.internationalthrillerreaders.com and click on the appropriate links.

ITW holds annual thriller conferences (details can be seen at www.thrillerfest.com) and in June 2006 its first anthology – Thriller, a collection of short stories by ITW members, was published to rave reviews. The collection received a $100,000 advance from its publisher. ITW is currently in the process of creating its own broadcasting network to promote its members' publications and thrillers in general.

The Crime Writers' Association (CWA)
PO Box 273,
Borehamwood WD6 2XA
Email: secretary@thecwa.co.uk

CWA membership is limited to published crime/thriller writers only. The Association holds regular events and invites interesting speakers such as police officers, forensic and medical experts, military personnel, legal experts, and so on. Members include John Le Carré, Ian Rankin and other notables. CWA runs various Dagger Award competitions, with prizes of up to £20,000.

The Society of Authors
84 Drayton Gardens,
London SW10 9SB
Tel: 020 7373 6642

The Society acts as a trade union for writers, campaigning on behalf of the profession and advising members on negotiating contracts with publishers, agents, theatre and film companies. It offers contract-vetting services and emergency funds for writers, and publishes a quarterly magazine *The Author.* Membership is open to published writers only.

The Writers' Guild of Great Britain
15 Britannia Street,
London WC1X 9JN
Tel: 020 7833 0777
Email: admin@writersguild.org.uk
Website: www.writersguild.co.uk

Founded in 1959, the Guild is another trade union for book, TV, radio, theatre and film writers. It offers many and diverse services to members, including contract negotiation and financial advice, help with copyright problems, representation in disputes with publishers, and so on. Various levels of membership are available, and unpublished authors may be eligible to join as Candidate or Student Members.

Academi
Mount Stuart House,
Mount Stuart Square,
Cardiff CF1 6DQ
Tel: 029 2047 2266
Website: www.academi.org

Academi is the national society for Welsh or Wales-based authors. Its members include major thriller authors Dick Francis and Ken Follett. Membership is open to all published writers resident in Wales. It provides advisory and mentoring services for writers and offers bursaries to support creative writing in Wales.

ARTS COUNCILS IN THE UK

Arts Council of England
14 Great Peter Street,
London SW1P 3NQ
Tel: 020 7333 0100
Website: www.artscouncil.org.uk

Welsh Arts Council
9 Museum Place,
Cardiff CF10 3NX
Tel: 029 2037 6500
Website: www.artswales.org.uk

Scottish Arts Council
12 Manor Place,
Edinburgh EH3 7DD
Tel: 0131 226 6051
Website: www.scottisharts.co.uk

Northern Ireland Arts Council
MacNiece House,
77 Malone Road,
Belfast BT9 6AQ
Tel: 028 900 385200
Website: www.artscouncil-ni.org

COURSES/SPECIALIST SERVICES FOR THRILLER WRITERS

Courses
In many guidebooks on writing, and in publications such as
The Writer's Handbook, you will come across long lists of

organisations, colleges and universities offering courses in creative writing either in-class or by distance learning/home study. Many of these courses may be excellent; however if your interest is to learn the art and craft of thriller-writing, before enrolling on any course it is wise to check two important points:

1. Does the course cover this subject? You may find that even if it does, it will only contain a very short module covering just the basics, and that much of the course deals with types of writing you might not be interested in. Many creative writing courses are heavily geared towards short story-writing, the more 'literary' end of full-length fiction, and poetry – perhaps good for the soul but not much use to the aspiring thriller writer.

2. Even more importantly, who are the tutors? Have they published anything themselves? More to the point, have they published *thrillers* with a *proper commercial* publisher? When calling for information, be politely firm on this – ask for names, titles and publishers, and check any details you are given.

More than one creative writing school I contacted refused to tell me the name of the course author or tutor. There can only be one valid reason for this: that the course has most likely been written, and is most likely taught, by someone who has never published anything commercially, at least not in this genre. Consider carefully whether signing up to such a course would be money well spent!

Other services

Writers' magazines are crammed with adverts for companies offering editorial, manuscript assessment and advisory services to writers as an intermediary step before approaching an agent or publisher. These services are run by former editors and agents, freelance publishers' readers, and – such as the one I run – commercially published authors. If you are thinking of approaching one of these companies for help and advice on your thriller project, make sure that the person assessing your manuscript is a suitably qualified expert with specialised knowledge of the genre.

CONTACTING THE AUTHOR

Scott Mariani can be contacted on:
+44 (0)1267 281761

www.scottmariani.com

Index